# Reviews for the Writings of Jerry D. Coleman

Jerry Coleman's investigations are second to none, leaving no stone unturned which translates to; always interesting, informative and seriously seeking the facts!

**Dr. Jim Lowery --- APSR Paranormal Talk Radio**

True researchers of paranormal phenomena, i.e, unknown animals, ghosts and the occult, are as rare as Bigfoot. In a field where the majority of books simply re-hash pre-existing data, myth, and urban legend, often with an eye toward the spectacular that ends up with mixed and conflicting results, "Strange Highways" is the exception. "Strange Highways" is a masterful compendium of his years of in-depth investigations across this country. He does not encumber his readers with wild speculation, or far-reaching conclusions that ultimately leave the reader shaking their heads in disbelief and disappointment. He is simply trying to shine a light on a truth that is far more often stranger than any fiction, and truly fascinating.

**Lee Murphy --- Author "Where Legends Roam"**

"Strange Highways" is a must-have for every strange phenomena fan. Cryptozoologists will learn, for the first time, the truth behind some of the best known cases in the field, including the Lawndale Big Bird Case; the Decatur, Illinois "North American Ape" tracks; the checkered history of Bigfoot; and much more. This book is a breath of fresh air and is guaranted to create huge ripples. Jerry D. Coleman has been on the inside of the strange phenomena sub-culture for decades and this book is long overdue! If you have an interest in the unexplained ... you will be shocked, surprised and enlightened by the revelations included in "Strange Highways".

**Mark Chorvinsky --- Veteran Investigator & Editor of Strange Magazine**

Jerry D. Coleman is one of the best-kept secrets in strange phenomena! He has been active investigating this field for more than three decades but has managed to stay quiet (until now) about the bizarre and unusual accounts and information that he had collected. Finally, he reveals the real, behind the scenes stories of some of America's greatest unexplained cases.

**Troy Taylor --- Author & Ghost Researcher**

This book is dedicated to my children: Jerry Denton, Jennifer Lynne, Stephanie Renee, Nicholas Dustin and Tara Whitney. I'm proud and fortunate to have ever had them in my life! Unbeknownst to them they are the central reason I have always tried my best to succeed, achieve and maintain a higher personal and professional standard.

I wish to also add a special dedication to the late Mark Chorvinsky (1954-2005) a respected Cryptozoology / Fortean researcher, Chief Editor of Strange Magazine and close personal friend. Mark's professional integrity and devotion shined blindly bright throughout his research years!

## - FURTHER EXPLORATIONS ON AMERICA'S DARK SIDE -

# MORE STRANGE HIGHWAYS

## MORE TRUE STORIES OF AMERICA'S UNKNOWN CREATURES & MYSTERIOUS HAPPENINGS
# BY JERRY D. COLEMAN

- A WHITECHAPEL PRODUCTIONS PRESS PUBLICATION -

Original Cover Artwork Designed by

This Book is Published by:
Whitechapel Productions Press
A Division of Ghosts of the Prairie
15 Forest Knolls Estates - Decatur, Illinois - 62521
(217) 422-1002 / 1-888-GHOSTLY
Visit us on the Internet at http://www.prairieghosts.com

First Edition - January 2006
ISBN: 1-892523-42-6

Printed in the United States of America

# TABLE OF CONTENTS

# 1. CREATURES THAT CROSS THE LINE

**N**ot all unexplained encounters are strange frightening creatures living deep in the forest, slithering through the swamps, lurking from the abyss of our lakes or casting enormous shadows from above and not all strange creatures nonchalantly appear and disappear merely for our personal amusement. Some of these unknown creatures and strange events seemingly interact with us as they cross the line of our reality.

Do things exist in the world we cannot explain, may not comprehend and even cannot see yet know or honestly believe they are there? Is it possible the unknown is as real as the invisible wind in your face or the silent radio waves bouncing off your body? As these unique events are presented, and the encounters retold, actuality will prevail over hype. Nevertheless, events to some are coincidence to others and a sighting of an unknown is an automatic misidentification to many. Often we leap too quickly to extraordinary conclusions when the need for an answer surpasses our common sense and logic.

These bizarre tales of creatures and other outlandish events often times becomes a never ending circle of mystery; sometimes revealing a pattern, a meaning or even a possible motive to a larger source rarely if ever contemplated. Fantastic explanations for those who remain unbiased. Unbiased, how easy to spout this state of mind that requires a discipline many claim, most aim for but few truly exhibit. However, when one is willing to examine creatures that apparently cross the line, often an investigation might go full circle --- returning to reality!

## Clara's Rape: The "New" Old Hag Syndrome

This phenomenon originates from a centuries old superstitious belief that a witch otherwise known as an "old hag", sits or lays on the chest of the victims, rendering them immobile. The instant, unpredictable occurrence is so swift and severe that it leads many people to believe supernatural forces transforming to demons are responsible. The episode is so frightening because the victims, although paralyzed, are completely aware of their surroundings and have full use of their senses. An old hag victim may experience any or all of the following; strange smells, glowing eyes, footsteps, shadows and the unbearable pressure on the chest, making breathing labored or almost impossible. The event ends as quickly as it began, often leaving the victim unconscious.

However, it appears that this strange, often interacting entity has taken on a new "look". Recent descriptions of old hag encounters are quite different from the once harmless, yet frightening, old England stories of an evil force that puts pressure on the chest, coupled with temporally paralyzing its victim. Today these stories that may only be classified as old hag-type encounters have been much more involved, long lasting, more intense and very personal as Clara, our witness would testify to.

It was in January of 2004 when I first met "Clara", a 35-year-old professional woman and mother of two. Clara was originally found when I was contacted by a man that had read "Strange Highways" and felt Clara's encounters might be of interest. Clara is an attractive woman; she is far from a religious fanatic and further from a substance-using individual. She maintains a nice home, holds down a prestigious job, is well-educated and devoted to her children. Clara demanded that her real name be kept secret, then willingly accepted the interview and freely told me of the strange and personally upsetting events that have been occurring to her over the past three years.

It first started, Clara recalls, in the fall of 2001. The day's activities were nothing out of the ordinary --- she went to work, stopped at Wal-Mart, checked the mail when she got home and was taking a breather before the bus would drop off her kids from school. As she eased, back in the recliner her left shoe fell off on its own. Thinking little of this, she reached down to take off the other when the shoe that was still on her foot forcefully flew across the room! Startled she attempted to jump up but realized she could not move. She said, "It was like something was holding me down, I couldn't even move my legs!" For what seemed like many minutes, all she could do was move her eyes around the room, her breathing was labored due to what felt like a heavy weight resting upon her chest and now her legs, arms and hands were totally immobile. Suddenly the air brakes of the school bus were heard and all returned to normal. She jumped up and went to meet her boys at the door. Clara quickly put the strange experience out of her mind and chalked it up to a weird short nap. Nevertheless, her flying shoe she stated was found 20 feet away in a planter.

Nothing more out of the ordinary happened for months; in fact, the entire shoe-flying episode was soon completely forgotten. It was not until the spring of 2002, while on her day off, that she planned to get her flowerbed planted. After acquiring the needed supplies and having a simple lunch, Clara proceeded to the flower garden in the rear of the yard. First, preparing to work the area soil, she went to the shed for tools, whena strange, strong odor was smelled, and then goose bumps engulfed her. She literally backed out of the shed and plopped down onto an awaiting lawn swing. Overcome with an evil unknown presence, Clara laid back in the swing. She could not move and could hardly breathe. Her blouse broke open as if ripped with one motion. Clara said, "I felt helpless and terrified, I couldn't move a muscle. I know I was wide awake this time as I watched the clouds and birds fly over." She continued, "Then the swing began to sway back and forth, my breathing was shallow and nothing I tried to move would move, other than my eyes, not even a finger." Clara told me it was as if she was pinned down and felt multiple hands racing across her body. Then as fast as it had begun, it was over. The swing stopped dead, the pressure was gone, and her breathing became normal but her blouse was still ripped.

Now, seriously frightened and connecting this new strange event to the afternoon in the recliner, Clara felt hopelessly and totally out of control. Immediately, she called her father in a panic and he raced over to her house to check the shed out and comfort her. Her dad found nothing but insisted she either go to the doctor, take a vacation or that her and the boys come stay with him for awhile, better yet he said, do all three. She accommodated his fatherly demands. The doctor found nothing physically wrong and the vacation and two week stay at her dad's appeared to bring all things back to normal. Clara and her father reasoned out the latest events as a simple case of the shed's chemical odors overcoming her, then Clara unconsciously tearing her blouse open to breath as she laid down on the swing. This gave the event a logical and acceptable excuse that she found comforting.

For Clara all seemed a little strange but once again was peaceful. Almost a year went passed without incident, no weird goings on, no trouble breathing and no paralyzing episodes. Clara recalls, "The furthest thoughts from my mind were the bizarre accounts I had experienced but as I got out of the bathtub one day, it all came roaring back."

Clara's boys were in the other room watching television as she climbed out of the tub and put her robe on. As she reached under the sink for the hair dryer, the bathroom lights went out. Going towards the door, she tripped and as she attempted to get up, an extremely heavy pressure rested on her chest and legs. She could not move and she could not see anything in the dark of the room,except for a streaking beam of light darting about the bathroom. She could hear the kids laughing at the television program but could not call out. Her robe now lay open and again, just as in the swing, she felt a swarm of hands moving across her entire body. Her arms like her legs, right down to her toes, were immobile. The beam of light hung over her, the hands felt rough and rapid and the darkness added more horror.

She lowered her head during the interview and said, "I have never told anyone this and I plan to never speak of it again but it, the light, the thing, it totally violated me."

I said, "You mean it...."

She interrupted me and blurted out, "Yes, I felt it inside me!" Clara then started break down, her voice cracked, tears streamed down her cheeks and she excused herself to gain composure. Minutes later, she returned and said, "You know I can't understand any of this, I've never seen a ghost, in fact I never really believed in them, I don't understand what's going on!"

I started to tell her about the "old hag syndrome" when she abruptly stopped me and said, "I was raped! This thing raped me! That's what it wanted all along, but why, why me!"

8

### Clara's Case: Conclusion

At the time of this writing, Clara has not experienced another encounter of any kind. She believes her visitor(s) purpose apparently attained its goal when it crossed the line.

After my interview with her, an added sense of duty drove me to contact a rape counselor volunteer. The volunteer reported, "After checking on Clara a few times, the lady does have all the symptoms of a rape victim and has come a long way to putting it behind her."

Now the question that needs asked is: was Clara's rape in truth a suppressed actual rape from the past? A rape her mind blocked out? A horrendous event she could not deal with in any form, other than to believe an evil entity had crossed the line?

Research confirms an untold number of rape victims are reluctant to come forward, so would not a rape victim of an evil entity be just as reluctant? One reasonable conclusion: Clara believes she was violated. Now whether it was a simple dream state, actual suppressed crime or an unlikely paranormal encounter, Clara had to confront her demons!

# Road Trolls

What creature lurks along our interstates, questioning our logic and testing our nerves? Could there exist an unknown 6 to 7 foot tall hairy, wild, nasty looking creature seen along our roadways many have claimed has a wooden peg-leg? A human-like figure so disgusting that a short glimpse of its strange appearance sends the witness into an internal debate as to what they just saw?

From 1981 to 2003, Road Troll sightings have been personally acquired by this author documenting 11 different locations throughout the southern and midwestern United States, some with multiple eyewitness testimony. In this section, many of the cases will be made public for the first time. These cases are unique and strange. Some day they are nothing more than urban legends of a peg-legged Bigfoot, while others claims the Road Troll is some kind of protector, spirit or ghost?

Most sightings of Road Trolls are reported by over-the-road long haul truck drivers. This is logical to me, since these individuals log millions of miles a year. However, first out of the mouths of many hardcore skeptics are these following arguments used only to ignore and debunk the sightings of Road Trolls.

Comments inlcude: all truck drivers use "road candy", (that is to say an illegal drug called speed). Then comes this generalized thought that the long late nights of driving while deprived of sleep is the simple explanation for the encounters. These two conditions do indeed contribute to hallucinations, however as true as it may be, these assumptions demand this question --- how is it that each professional driver tells such similar story?

The close-minded skeptic quickly goes to yet another popularly accepted conclusion, that truckers love to tell a tall tale and have the time to think it up. They also have access to one another to compare notes, thus, evidently surmising a center-white-line hypnoses causes the need to make up such events. I doubt this is true in many (if any) of the cases, but I will not conclude that the hardcore skeptics are completely off base.

I've been around truckers since 1981 (being one myself in the early 1980's then again hitting the road in the 1990's), which gave proof to the fact that I never heard tall tales being used to fool a fellow trucker with make believe road monsters. When such a story was were heard, it was always sincere in nature and voluntarily initiated and told privately in coffee shops or loading docks, not blasted over the C.B. radio, as some would claim! If these types of incredible tales got back to their dispatch the driver may be, up for discipline via logbook violations, (driving on deprived sleep), immediately drug tested and / or simply taken off the truck.

The days and laws have change tremendously since the liberal 1960's and loose 1970's. Granted, a few "road rebel's" still fly up and down the interstates and do tell tall tales to total strangers but these tales often refer to one or two blond babes that beg fat, bald, haven't-taken-a-shower-for-two-weeks driver for a ride and companionship. Or another, often told tall truck driver tale that reflects a version of a short day's run, which paid five times what others get and usually is but a one pallet light load! These types of fibs are spotted a mile away and are a sure sign of lonely drivers on an ego trip, rather than a road trip. Lies of legendary road monsters by truck drivers? This is just not the answer here.

If one insists on sticking to their theory of drivers seeing Road Trolls due to hallucinations, then address this next question: how is it that even some short run drivers, drivers that have just began their trip (which are well rested and drug tested) have seen and reported these Road Trolls? But more importantly, how would the hardcore skeptics explain away such cases as the mother of two, headed to the mall or the pastor going to a church gathering, both who claim an encounter with a Road Troll? These latter two cases are not alleged drug-taking truck drivers, deprived of sleep and spinning yarns. They are average citizens out on what was thought to be average trip.

### The Green Pond Road Troll
In 1983, I interviewed a woman we can only refer to as "Barb" (and at her request, we'll hold her last name for privacy). While sitting at her kitchen table in Des Plaines, Illinois, she told me of a trip taken to Alabama to visit her sister. The automobile trip went without a hitch. She was well rested and only excited about reminiscing with her sibling. On the day following her arrival, an early morning journey was underway to a Birmingham strip-mall.

On their way to the mall, located on I-20 and I-59 by Green Pond (mile marker 97 by a weigh station) her sister exclaimed, "What the hell is that!" Quickly Barb slowed down and followed her sister's eye to the road's edge in front of them. Now going just under 30 miles an hour, they passed what appeared to be a wild looking man (?) Immediately, the chatting and laughter in the car was replaced with total silence. Barb's eye's locked on the creature and her sister stared into the rearview mirror as they passed the unorthodox-looking figure.

Barb told me the creature was much taller than her husband (he is 5'10"), it had hair at least a foot long covering its face and its clothes looked like what one may think clothes would look like if a car dragged them. She continued, "The man, or whatever it was, just looked at us, a look of curiosity I'd call it. We both agreed it had a wooden leg or walking stick in front of its leg --- we were not sure." Barb then said, "I felt guilty that we didn't call the police to check it out."

I interviewed Barb again while writing this account. Now, years later, she continues to stick to her story that the day she and her sister saw that "thing" outside of Birmingham, Alabama was one of the strangest days of her life. She added, "After seeing the creature, or whatever it was, it totally changed our plans."

I asked her to elaborate, and Barb continued, "We didn't go on to the mall as planned, instead, so shaken and concerned, we stopped at a nearby coffee shop and quietly sat composing ourselves and caught up on sister talk and.... never mind you'll think I'm silly."

I insisted, "Please continue."

Barb then said, "I never told you this, never thought it was related to the sighting but when we returned home, three hours earlier than we had planned, my sister's son had fallen out of a tree he was climbing. The babysitter was getting ice when we walked in, but her son's bone was exposed and we rushed him to the emergency room. In retrospect, I've always felt if we hadn't seen that 'thing' and returned home, maybe her son would have laid there and bled to death."

### Truckers Road Troll's

Professional drivers, Gary Durbin, Adam Sanders and Adam's father's sightings are well documented in my book "Strange Highways". The Durbin and the Sanders encounters were years and states apart, from Florida to Texas in 1981 to 2003, yet both parties explained, almost in identical detail their Road Troll stories. So too, did another truck driver I interviewed south of Dallas, Texas.

In the winter of 2000, I had the opportunity to interview a person who asked I only use his CB handle name, which was "Gunslinger". Gunslinger and I were in a truck-stop just south of Dallas / Fort Worth sharing a pot of coffee as he told me tales of his road life. Gunslinger spoke of many unique and interesting experiences but one story caught my attention. It was a story I had heard many times before --- an encounter of a large hairy peg-legged wild-man. (Note: Gunslinger had no clue of my connection with Cryptozoological and Paranormal research).

Gunslinger told me that on February the 27, 1998, around 4 or 4:30 p.m., he was driving on I-255 after loading in Saint Louis and was headed for Chicago. As he approached the junction of I-255 and I-270, 12 to 14 miles from Alton, Illinois and 4 miles north of the Collinsville weigh station, he spotted a figure along the road.

Slowing down, in fact as he put it, "I took my foot out of the carburetor and threw on the Jake-break, not knowing if the thing was going to cross the road." He recalls the date and time so well because he still carries the log-book in the sleeper of his present truck and insisted I follow him to the truck so he could show me the notes written in the margins, which confirmed the testimony. In the margin read, "Strange wild looking man seen", on the reverse of the log book read, "This thing was big, hairy and almost looked fake until it moved!"

Gunslinger's description of the varmint was as follows: "It stood well over 6 foot tall, maybe even 7 foot tall, long hair that covered its face and arms, the creature had a peg-leg just below the right knee and was wearing very out of date, torn-up clothes." He added these observations, "It didn't move until the truck got right up to it, I was going fairly slow and got an excellent look at it. I honestly didn't think it was real but then it turned its head and looked my way! I'm not sure what I saw, thoughts of a wild, weird creature quickly crossed my mind, I am sure it was no ordinary hitchhiking man!"

Another report by Brad Royalty (an owner/operator) stated that on March 15, 2000, he also apparently spotted a peculiar pedestrian. Royalty claims he spotted a peg-legged Road Troll standing along I-44 outside of Big Cabin, Oklahoma. Royalty stated, "The thing was tall and hairy and had a wooden leg, I first thought it was a bum but it freaked me out, it just stared".

Another report from Doug and his wife (also an owner/operator team), stated that they too saw what seemed to be a peg-legged Road Troll sometime in the mid-summer months of 2000. It was on I-70 by Boonville, Missouri, just one mile from a rest area. Doug reported: "The man, or whatever it was, didn't even act like he was hitchhiking or doing anything. No vehicles were broken down within miles, and to be honest it looked like a huge scarecrow, it had an artificial leg and a lot of hair!" His wife refused to comment, other than saying, "It scared me to death!"

### The Pastor's Road Troll

Another sighting was reported by Pastor Jim Washington of East Tennessee. Pastor Jim was on his way to a church function on the evening of June 4, 2003, around 7:15 p.m. The Pastor was taking an all too familiar route down I-181 south of Johnson City, Tennessee to the small town of Erwin. Just outside the town of Unicoi, he spied a large, hairy, crippled man (?) along the interstate shoulder. Concerned about the individual, he took the next exit and returned to the location where he had seen the unkempt-looking thing, but nothing was found. It had disappeared.

The Pastor stated, "I felt sorry for him and wanted to help if I could, so I turned the car around. Although it took me 2 or 3 minutes to get turned around, he was long gone. He was so wild and strange-looking with an obvious disfigurement of the leg that I can't imagine anyone picking him up. Then the Pastor added this final thought, "I can't explain it but he appeared lost."

Further examination of this event and the location uncovered little other than a closely related report of a Bigfoot-like creature seen near Erwin, Tennessee two weeks later.

# Road Troll Cases 1981 Through 2003

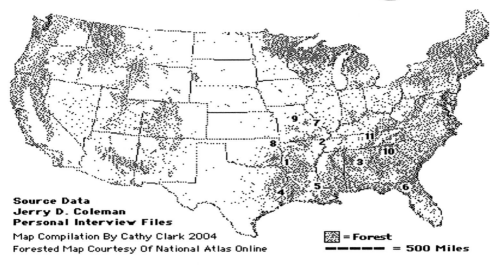

Source Data
Jerry D. Coleman
Personal Interview Files
Map Compilation By Cathy Clark 2004
Forested Map Courtesy Of National Atlas Online

▨ = Forest
━━━━ = 500 Miles

## Road Troll Sightings as marked on map, note the close proximity to forests:

1. 1981 Little Rock, Arkansas - East of Ouachita National Forest
2. 1981 Cooter, Missouri - South of Mark Twain National Forest
3. 1983 Birmingham, Alabama - West of Talladega National Forest
4. 1984 Huntsville, Texas - San Jacinto/Sam Houston National Forest
5. 1986 Natchez, Mississippi - Homochitto National Forest
6. 1991 Live Oak, Florida - Osceola National Forest
7. 1998  South of Alton, Illinois - Northwest of Shawnee National Forest / South of Mississippi River Fish & Wildlife Area.
8. 2000 Big Cabin, Oklahoma - North of Cherokee State Park
9. 2000 Boonville, Missouri - Katy Trail State Park
10. 2003 Carnesville, Georgia - South of Chattahoochee National Forest
11. 2003 Johnson City, Tennessee - North of Cherokee National Forest

### The Road Troll Theories

The 10 witnesses we have examined all have similar stories. These tes-timonies came from professional truck drivers, their passengers, a home-maker, her sister and a pastor and span 22 years, stretching from Florida to Texas into Missouri, Illinois and Tennessee. Are these to be considered only lies, coincidences or hallucinations? Doubtful. What is it these people are truly seeing?

One theory quietly kicked around of Road Trolls is that these tattered old-time-clothes-wearing hairy homo anomalous' originate from the ancient story of protective guards. In this theory, Cortez's army, while fleeing north and hiding Aztec Treasure in the southwestern deserts, left slaves behind armed with flintlock rifles to guard the treasure. This story appears to transform the wooden leg (or walking stick) witnesses have testified seeing into a musket. However, it does not explain the sightings found in the southeast and mid-western United States.

Another theory accepted by some is that these Road Troll sightings are in truth, a Peg-legged Bigfoot. In this theory, the torn clothing is actually matted hair. In most cases, the locations of the sightings coincide with other Bigfoot reports. A Bigfoot with an artificial limb? Seems very illogical!

More likely, it may be a simple case of a traveling soul, a feral human that finds the establishment an unnecessary infringement on his life. He may be simply an unkempt individual of uncommon stature who is wishing to escape the taxman and the time clock.

I recall in the winter of 1984, while on my way to work the graveyard shift, I would pass a secluded wooded area and notice movement around a small campfire. After days of passing this activity, curiosity got the best of me. Stopping along the shoulder of the highway (route 19 by Elgin, Illinois), I hiked back to the 'camp' and there sat a large young man of 21 peacefully eating some cornflakes. His appearance was quite frightening. The hair atop his head was extremely long, matted and wild looking. His facial hair was long and patchy, his clothes appeared torn and tattered and his odor was unbearable. He told me his parents had both recently died and left him a huge fortune. He said that distant family members started coming out of the woodwork, lawyers had unwanted advice and neighbors who had never met his parents were now taking interest in him. He had to get away and think things out --- and of course, to mourn in peace. I questioned his method but understood completely. Later that day, a police buddy of mine was called upon to check in on him from time to time. Three months later, the young man and the campsite had disappeared. Could the Road Troll be someone, several someones, in a similar situation?

Or are these sightings a peg-legged Bigfoot? Alternatively, loyal spirits still standing guard? Who knows, but perhaps it is an unknown entity of our mind an unexplained "homo anomalous" with little purpose, playing cosmic games, or with a lot of purpose, changing fate to those who see it? Does the witness think they see something, thus stimulating or alerting these drivers back to reality, when their minds may have drifted from the task at hand. Or as in Barb and the pastor's case, an obvious detour in the direct path of travel, possible delaying them and others, avoiding an accident awaiting around the next curve of changeable fate?

## *Gnomes of the Night Hours*

These unbelievable creatures called gnomes, goblins or dwarfs have been thought of for centuries as guardians to our earth's subterranean treasures. More recent beliefs place gnomes right in your house, in your closest or even in the tool shed! Are these gnomes doing silly little deeds or simply there to be seen, then quickly disappearing? Sighting or experiencing a gnome is a complete self or group interpretation. These small human-like, deformed entities must be conjured up due to a conscious or unconscious attempt to give reason to a shadow or a mislabeling of an actual event --- or are they? Gnomes are most often seen by children and explained in an uncanny detailed description. Gnomes are no true life form, rarely look alike from case to case, leave no physical evidence behind and seldom if ever speak or physically interact.

Although a gnome is thought to be an imaginary being, can we ignore the encounters and throw out the testimony? Or should we study the events and sort out the stories? After all, aren't ghosts in essence the same in character as these gnomes? I must ask what and how, even why, do these children see these beings and explain them in such remarkably similar ways?

### Case in Point:
In August 2003, I interviewed Jason Harron (age 16) of Church Hill, Tennessee about his alleged experience with a gnome. Although the event took place over eight years ago, Jason recalled the encounter in apparent precise detail and still appeared very emotional in the telling of it.

Eight years before, in the winter of 1995, Jason was helping his mother's boyfriend, "Donald" work on her broken-down car. Jason was the "gopher", running back and forth to the tool shed and getting tools at Donald's request. It was a Wednesday afternoon and school had been cancelled due to a snowfall, which powdered the ground. Soon, the late afternoon turned into nightfall and the car seemed no closer to being fixed than it was hours earlier.

Jason, carrying a flashlight, went to the shed and flipped the light on inside and started looking for an extension cord and droplight, per Donald's request. Soon, he found an extension cord but continued his search for the droplight when a loud bang was heard, spinning him around 180 degrees. A large metal tub had fell off its hanger revealing the droplight that had been hidden underneath. Thinking nothing of it, he grabbed the light and ran back to the automobile.

A few minutes later, Jason was asked to go get a crowbar. Donald told Jason exactly where the tool should be lying, adding, "I know it's under the tool bench".

Strolling to the shed, Jason noticed the door was closed. The inside light was out but the exterior light above the door remained on. He had left the door open all day and knew he didn't close it, nor did he recall turning the light off but reasoned the wind must have closed the door and maybe he did unconsciously flip the light out. He charged into the shed and turned the light back on and began searching for the crowbar but couldn't find it. Jason then stood-up on his tip-toes to look out the window and tap on it to get his co-workers attention. It was then that Jason claims to have seen the top of someone's head race by the window!

Scared and unnerved, he ran out of the shed and told Donald he could not find the crowbar. Donald said, "Come with me, I'll show you where it is."

A quick search revealed no crowbar, but as Donald stood there scratching his head a thud was heard at the rear of the shed. Donald and Jason went to check out the noise and found the crowbar lying next to the back outside wall of the shed.

Donald snapped at Jason, "What kind of game are you playing?"

Jason replied, "I saw someone go past the window, they must have taken it?"

Donald, not believing Jason's story, pacified him anyway with a search for footprints. All they found however was was a line in the snow where it appeared the crowbar had been dragged to the rear of the building.

Returning to the car, Donald told Jason he did not appreciate his games and Jason kept repeating he did not do anything. A few minutes passed then again Donald asked Jason to go in the shed and get the electrical tape, adding, "I KNOW it's on the workbench, I just saw it!"

Jason reluctantly once again headed for the tool shed. Slowly walking with eyes locked on the building, he was about half way there when the light inside went out. Jason yelled, "I can't go in there" and ran into the house.

Now safe in the house, Jason watched out the window of his bedroom. Donald was now in the shed looking for the tape. Jason stated that it was at this time that he saw a small shadow-like human figure walking to the car. He described the thing as being about 4 foot tall; wearing what looked like a long dark coat and a small, strange looking little hat. Once the shadow reached the car, it seemed to vanish in thin air!

Donald couldn't find the tape and came out of the shed screaming at the top of his lungs for Jason to bring him the tape! Walking towards the car, Donald was still yelling for Jason when he saw the tape lying on the fender. Donald picked up the tape and went into the house to have a few words with the "prankster". Jason denied all of Donald's accusations --- and continues to do so to this day!

### Speculative Remarks of the Gnomes of the Night Hours:

After my interview with him, I found no reason for Jason to lie or make up such a tale. But I had to ask if Donald could have been the prankster? Donald said he knew where the crowbar was and could have easily grabbed the tape while pretending to search for the crowbar. All it would have taken is an accomplice and a very little bit of planning to pull it off.

The metal tub that fell revealing the droplight may have had some fishing line connected to it, thus starting the hoax. I did find old fishing line still hanging from the ceiling in the shed. The crowbar may have been placed behind the shed earlier that day. During my examination of the utility building it was noted that no rain gutters were on the roof's edge and I surmised that the line believed to be that of the crowbar being dragged may have been nothing more than a line of melting roof snow. The fact that no footsteps were found of Jason's little creature might have been due to Donald carefully and consciously walking over the top of them. Donald scratching his head while in the shed may have been a signal to his co-conspirator to toss a rock or a distraction so he could throw a small item against the rear wall himself, thus making it appear to be the sound of a crowbar falling against the back wall. The tape could have been easily picked up and placed on the fender by Donald himself. The shadowy figure going to the car then vanishing again was possibly our unknown hoax-helper, who then ducked behind the vehicle, scaring Jason away from the window --- only to then be distracted by the seemingly angry Donald.

This is total speculation on my part and is only a method outlined of how these events could have been hoaxed. The speculation is teaming with maybe's, if's and's and but's. In any case, now that we have established opportunity and method, one must now ask motive and personality of the perpetrator (s).

Jason told me Donald was a serious individual, nice, polite but never one to play games. It did trouble me a bit that Donald refused the use of his name in this account, stating that it was for personal reasons, but this honestly has no bearing on the case, or does it? Being an over-the-road truck driver who only knew a few people in the area, it's doubtful that Donald could have enlisted a neighborhood kid to not only assist him in the prank but also keep his mouth closed about this premeditated fraud. Donald never revealed that a joke ever took place. In addition, he would would have had to know in advance that Jason would be helping him well after dark and that the car would not be repaired. The mother, Donald's girlfriend, was stranded at her mother's house and needed a ride home; making it very doubtful Donald would have stretched out the repair job for a child's prank.

Donald, Jason later stated, could not have walked over any footprints because when they went to the rear of the shed and found the crowbar, they had circled it from the other side and only when we searched for foot tracks did they go to the window side of the structure. He could plainly see no foot prints in the snow where he had just seen a figure run by.

Of course, there is this possibility: The tub coincidently fell, sparking the initial thoughts of strangeness. The crowbar was never under the tool table to begin with. Donald, a little bit frustrated, unconsciously grabbed the tape and placed it on the fender. Jason, thinking he saw a person walk past the window, might have seen the glance of an evening owl or another bird seen frequently around out buildings. Therefore, our bird would explain why there were no prints in the snow and could even explain the sound heard at the rear of the tool shed. The light going off for the second time as he approached may have been faulty wiring or a blown bulb. By the time he went inside, Jason was frightened and he could have seen Donald's shadow cast from the outside, or inside, shed light onto or near the car or it may have been complete imagination at this point.

Now, let us take yet a third and final possibility to Jason's gnome. Looking at the simple facts, we have Jason at age eight; no school that day, no friends over, bored and helping a man he finds nice but not entertaining, doing the meager task of running for tools all day outside in the chill of winter. At some point, at least fleetingly, young Jason must have thought wouldn't it be nice to have a friend over or a younger brother to send for these tools? Is it possible Jason himself created the gnome or mentally invited it in some way to exist alongside of him for those few minutes?

Researcher David Evans of Cardiff, Wales in the UK may have put it best with his reference to the Tulpa theory of Tibet. In this theory, the method involved was essentially intense concentration and visualization. An experiment subject's "tulpa" (a mind-created creature) began its existence as a plump, benign little monk, similar to Friar Tuck. It was at first entirely subjective, but gradually, with practice, she was able to visualize the tulpa like an imaginary ghost flitting about the real world. In time, the vision grew in clarity and substance until it was indistinguishable from physical reality ----a sort of self-induced hallucination. But the day came when the hallucination slipped from her conscious control. She discovered that the monk would appear from time to time when she had not willed it. Furthermore, her friendly little figure was slimming down and taking on a distinctly sinister aspect. ( Tulpa source:  **http://www.tulpa.com/explain/alexandra.html** ).

Whatever actually occurred in that Tennessee toolshed that night ----one thing is for certain, Jason Harron believes he saw a gnome!

# 2. ENIGMATIC ENTITIES CALLED GHOSTS

In the following stories, which have become accepted local legends rather than a present-day search for the unknown, one must consider this: how witnesses report, believe and apparently assume events, filling in the blanks and creating a mystery where indeed truth may have its roots. Are testimonies molded to fit the legend, or is it possible these strange events are being reported with much more accuracy then one dares to believe?

East Tennessee and western Virginia are thick as a London fog with unwritten tales of ghostly slaves. As a descendant of the Cherokee Nation, my interest in suppressed people has always been a part of my make-up but it peaked after reading Troy Taylor's book *Spirits of the Civil War.* After completing his book, as if on cue, an acquaintance told me about a stone wall built by slaves and graciously escorted me to the location.

Soon, the horrible tales, which are more numerous and colder than the stones of the wall, were retold to me by the locals. Some witnesses claimed the eerie sounds at night are the slave cries from the rock wall they built, a wall that still stands today as a grim reminder of the horror, torture and death it caused to construct it.

## THE SLAVE WALL

As I went door to door, tales about the stone wall were recounted but no one seemed to recall any details, only anecdotes. That was until I found and interviewed an old man who claimed to know the true story of a young slave called Pepper Smith. The man lived a half-mile down the road from the slave wall and told a tale of a 14 year-old slave boy named Pepper Smith that had his left hand cut off at age 9 for stealing some "extra" eggs for his mother. The old man and I walked the wall as he narrated the 100 year-old saga of Pepper Smith.

Years ago, the plantation owner demanded his slaves continually clear the fields of rocks but became obsessed with building a wall from these stones and insisted each slave pull his weight or face harsh punishment. Pepper overcame his handicap and carried more rocks from the field to the wall than any of the strongest men could. He accomplished this by tying a rope around a wire hoop to lift or drag the stone. This was a task not done for the Master, Pepper did it for pure self-pride. One day while out in the field working and being eaten alive by bugs, Pepper decided to run away. He knew the Master went into the house daily for dinner around six o'clock and this would be his window of escape. It would give him a good hour to get well down the road and deep into the woods, maybe even longer if a head count wasn't done upon the Master's return from dinner.

Young Pepper Smith knew his biggest obstacle to maintain a successful getaway would be a supply of food, so for days Pepper and his family stock piled as much food as he felt could be carried. The escape day eventually came. Pepper found no reasons to postpone it any longer, so as the Master rode off to the house, he strolled over to the nearby wagon, grabbed his hidden supplies and took off. Delight mixed with fear came to his family and friends as they watched him scurry away and disappear into the woods. The Master returned after an hour and no head count was taken. Pepper was not missed until the group started the march back to the shacks by the barn. It was then that the Master yelled out to Pepper's mother, demanding that she tell him Pepper's whereabouts. The boy's mother, Maggie, said he had gone to the barn to clean the stalls. Satisfied with this explanation, the Master unknowingly gave Pepper the entire night to make his escape.

In the past, the Master had taken a branding iron to liar's tongues. Maggie and the others knew a good plan was needed for the morning when there would be no denying Pepper was gone. That evening, one of the women motioned to the Overseer's watchman to come into her shack. This gave provided the perfect alibi needed --- it must have been during this late night time when Pepper had slipped away.

After the Master discovered Pepper's disappearance, and swallowed the excuse, an immediate search party was formed. For the next five days and four nights, the search party came up empty but on the sixth day, they got word that a Negro boy had been spotted raiding a vegetable garden 20 miles to the north. This was all the posse needed to hear. By the next evening, Pepper was found, hog-tied, and brought back to the plantation.

The Master, wanting to make an example out of Pepper, tied him up by his armpits in the barn, raising him a few inches off the ground. For days, flies ate at his body and face and barn cats nibbled at his feet. At first he fought it but soon was too weak to care. Occasionally the Master would walk past and spit on him, laughing as he spooked the flies into flight.

Pepper never apologized for making his escape nor begged for his life. As the story goes, the Master was so frustrated with Pepper's defiance that he tried making a horse kick him.

But Pepper laughed in the Master's face and said, "I may die but I will not leave, you will never rid yourself of me now!"

So angered by the slave's words, the Master began beating the horse, which quickly turned on the Master, driving his head into a pole and crushing his skull.

Two days later, Pepper also died and according to the legend, he kept his word and never left the land. To this day, the locals claim that he still haunts the barn and walks the rock wall on foggy nights.

*The "Old Slave Wall", which divides hundreds of acres of Virginia farmland. In some places, the wall's base is greater than 12 feet wide and well over 7 feet high. Stones of the wall range in size from a youngster's fist to an elephants head, perhaps larger.*

## Present Day Tales of the Wall

With very little effort, one can find numerous tales of the slave wall. Some say they have seen groups of slaves still piling rocks on the wall and walking toward the barn at night, while others tell of screams and hear old squeaky wagons rolling across the field. One person even stated she had waved at a young black boy standing by the road one evening. She went on to say, "Right away, I noticed he didn't have a hand."

A young couple that lives in a trailer not a mile up the road from the wall swears, "Too many strange noises and unusual events take place around the wall to call it all fantasy." Paul and Teresa Cross claim it is more than the stories they hear, it is actual things they have seen and have heard for themselves.

Once, while taking an evening stroll, Teresa saw a young man walking towards the barn from the wall. She told me, "I couldn't see him very well at all. His back was to me most of the time, but I did see he had on real old looking clothes and didn't seem to be walking anywhere. I mean he walked a ways, picked up a rock, then walked a ways and did it again and again."

Teresa then said: "Another time I was out walking with my husband Paul, we had just got in front of the wall when we heard someone cough. We both quickly turned our heads to the left and saw a young boy sitting on the rock wall." She paused here and yelled for her husband to join us, then continued, "Paul remember the evening we saw the boy sitting on the wall? Tell Mr. Coleman about it."

Paul looked at me and said, "It was just a kid sitting on the wall. I figured he was waiting for a ride or going fishing or something but it was pretty weird. It was like he didn't see us and he was wearing heavy old wool pants. Strange...."

Then Teresa added: "When we came back by the wall, not five minutes later, the kid was gone and no cars had passed us."

Teresa ended the interview with this: "I don't know what is real or unreal over there by the wall. We hear strange whistles and moans, see shadows by the wall and at times by the barn, and it's just creepy."

## Emily Baker's Encounter

Another witness I found, Emily Baker, had quite a different tale of the stone wall. She's convinced that it's the Master who now haunts the old plantation. Mrs. Baker is a long time resident of the area. It was in 1968 that she and her husband moved into the home that offers a wonderful view of the countryside, including the slave wall, which can be seen from the dining room window. Over the years, Mrs. Baker states that on any given night unusual ghostly events can be seen.

Mrs. Baker said: "It was one summer evening in the early 1970's that I first became aware all was not peaceful at the rock wall." Her husband often worked the late shift at a local mine and was never expected home until after daylight. Mrs. Baker would get up at five a.m. to prepare her husband breakfast and fix herself up a bit, as she never knew if he would want to go directly to bed or into town.

One morning she got up as usual. While it was still dark out, she had taken the garbage out and heard a strange "tsk, tsk, tsk" sound. The sound would fade in and out with intensity and had no pattern to it. She paused to listen closer to it in the complete pitch black of the night. It was a tsk, then two loud tsk's, then nothing for a second, then more rapid weak tsk's coupled with what could only be described as laughter. All she was sure of was the direction from where the sound emulated --- it came from the wall. Uncomfortable but not frightened, she finished her chores and awaited her husbands arrival.  After he went to bed, just after daybreak, she strolled over to the wall, hoping something may explain the unusual sounds. She found nothing that could have caused them.

About a week passed and once again, she found herself outside taking the garbage to its container. This time, nothing was heard until she had started back to the house. The sound was definitely laughter.  She stopped, turned, and firmly yelled out, "Who's there?!"

No one answered but the laughter continued. Mrs. Baker then called again, "I'm going to get my husband and his shotgun!" There was still no answer and the tsk-ing sound started up again. This time, she admitted that she was quite shaken. She double-locked the doors and turned on all the exterior lights.

The following morning, she told her husband of the events and he had quite a laugh at her expense. He simply brushed it off as insects and her imaginationand it was then that Emily swore she would never breathe another word to him about anything else that might happen. She did not have to wait very long for something else to occur. Within the month, she again heard noises by the wall but this time they were quite different. She recalled that the tsk sounds seemed louder and "meaner". She could not explain what she meant by that it and was not sure she understood it herself.

The morning after the last incident, she was standing in the kitchen, fixing some eggs, and her husband called to her from the other room, looking for a clean pair of pants and a shirt. Emily picked up his filthy pants and jerked the belt from the loops. "That's it!" she exclaimed.

Her husband, confused, yelled back to her. "What?" he shouted. "What's it?"

She replied, "Oh nothing, nothing at all."

Little did she know this would create more questions than answers.

Days and weeks went past with no sounds but they eventually returned. A sudden crack of thunder sent Emily outside one evening to put the windows up in her car and the tsk-ing was heard behind her. She spun around and was looking directly at the stone wall. Another tsk was heard, then another and then the sounds were followed by the eerie silence of "the calm before the storm". She walked a few steps closer to the wall and heard what sounded like a man coughing. Then suddently, she heard the sound of that evil laughter from weeks before. She could see nothing from the distance though.

Taking a few deep breaths and getting the big flashlight out of her car trunk, she started walking. She later told me that, "I felt it had to be done. I was afraid but wasn't going to live my entire life wondering what the sounds were."

Emily cautiously stepped closer to the wall, waiting between the odd sounds, then taking a few more steps more.  Emily was all but on top of the wall and strangely, the sounds seemed to be moving at the same distance away from her as she approached. She finally reached the barrier of rocks and stood there waiting by an old oak tree --- and listening. Eerily, the laughter began coming towards her but Emily stood her ground. It came to within a few yards and then the strange tsk-ing sound came from directly over head and she began to feel what seemed like bugs dropping on her neck and arms. Emily let out a scream and dropping the flashlight, took off running to the house. She slammed the door shut behind her, locked it and took a gun to bed with her that night.

She felt stronger when daylight arrived and her husband was at home and tucked into bed. She gathered her courage and wandered out to the slave wall again. Emily found her flashlight right where she had dropped it and looked at the tree she had been standing under the night before.

She recalled tome: "You know what I thought were bugs landing on me? Well, it was small pieces of bark hitting me! Exactly where I was standing but higher, there were at least three fresh straight marks that had cleaned the bark right off the tree!"

Mrs. Baker glared at me and said, "I don't care if you believe me or not but I have a theory of my encounters." Then she added, "The sound, the tsk, was a whip, yes, it was a whip. I realized that the day I snapped the belt from my husbands trousers .... it was the identical sound!"

As of this writing, Mrs. Emily Baker and other locals are still witnessing strange events and hearing weird sounds from the slave's stone wall of Scott County, Virginia.

Emily told me that she preferred not to say too much more about her experiences with the wall, hoping that she might write her own book on the subject one day. However, on the day I interviewed her, she added one last thing about the wall as I was backing out of her drive. "One night," she said, "not two years ago, I heard some of the scream-like sounds, so I snapped a bunch of photographs in the direction of the wall and set up a tape recorder. You'd be amazed at what I caught. It'll be in my book if I decide to write one."

## The Laney's Interview --- The Stone Wall

As I drove up the quarter mile dirt drive to the Laney farm's barn, I found myself in awe of the monstrous wall, which stretched for acres and acres into the distance. Completely hidden from the main road, thanks to the summer foliage, the slave wall soon emerged, extending from one farm to the next. Jack Laney came roaring up to the barn on his ATV to get a tool needed in the field but was kind enough to stop for a few minutes and answer a few questions.

Jack was the co-owner of the farm with his father, Ray, and quickly confirmed that the wall was indeed constructed by the slaves of the long past owner, Mr. Hagan. When asked if he knew of any strange events or ghostly stories, Jack replied: "I'll tell you this much... as a child until now, and I'm in my 50's, I've spent many a day searching for the hidden cemetery of the slaves that built this wall. It's said to be in those mountains right behind you (as he motioned northeast). I know it's up there and someday I'll find it."

I asked Jack if he knew anymore of the history that went with the wall and he replied: "My dad, Ray, is 74 and could tell you a lot more than I can but one thing I do know is that the the last of the Hagan's was Pat. He also had slaves that continued to construct this wall. It went on for generations, with no generation ever seeing the finished wall. Pat Hagan would sit on the bank of Sulfur Creek drinking himself drunk on moonshine day after day,

*The author (left) during an on-site interview with Ray Laney. The "Slave Stone Wall" borders Laney's farm on all sides (May 2004)*

only to return in a rage because the wall had not progressed to his satisfaction."

Jack then added that he had to return to the field with his tool before an expected rainstorm but assured me that he would send his father us to the barn, who knew more of the history. He told me to feel free to walk around and photograph whatever I liked.

After a few minutes had passed, Ray Laney walked up another dirt road behind the barn. I introduced myself and Ray kindly jumped into the conversation with both feet. He told me about the lost cemetery that simply must exist and the stories of the Hagan's odd, life-long mission from one generation to the next to build the slave wall.

He had heard the rumors and legends of the "Blood Rock Slave Wall" and laughed off most all the ghostly sightings and strange events but did acknowledge and accept the strong possibility that many a slave lost their lives in the fields he and his neighbors now farm.

Ray Laney said: "The Hagan's once owned most of the land you can see in all directions, farming it, and continued building the wall with slaves long after the Civil War had ended."

Ray told me of the last known descendant of the Hagan's, a Jim Scott, now living in Gate City, Virginia. Ray also stated behind here that behind his was a place that they called Hunters Valley. There was an old lime mill that the slaves used to work and it was still intact. There were also a few log structures the slaves had lived in, now carpteted with weeds. The valley was kept locked and the owner lived in Knoxville. (Author's Note: As of this writing, I'm still working on getting access to this area)

Just as Ray and I parted company, Ray's granddaughter, Jessica Laney, came walking over to see who I was. Jessica was a senior in college had just returned from a swimming hole, dressed in a Confederate flag bikini. I felt it might be important to interview her as well.

Jessica told me that, throughout her life, she had heard stories of slaves that were buried under the wall and found no reason to disbelieve it. "My dad has searched for many years for the lost slave cemetery without success," she explained, "but I believe it's up there. It must be and should be found and marked properly."

Jessica Laney did not speak of any ghostly encounters or strange events but this investigator had a gut feeling she was not comfortable going into it.

Further research is going into this case. At this writing, I am precisely mapping out the entire structure and actively speaking with local historical societies to save and protect this area. Also, a request has been submitted to the government to find and mark the slave cemetery.

## Good Evening Mrs. Ball

One summer evening in mid-July of 2003, well past 10:00 p.m., a friend and I were sitting outside enjoying the night's breeze that eased its way through the sparsely populated valley in Church Hill, Tennessee. A couple of neighbors joined us and as the peaceful talk drifted from one subject to the next, and the sweet tea was tasting better with each gulp, one of the guests, Chad Gillenwater, asked to see my large spotlight I kept in the truck. He was amazed at its brightness, but I suggested the only way to appreciate its candle power of 200,000, and powerful piercing beam, was to take a quick ride over to the mountain to Cooper Cemetery. The cemetery was no more than a half-mile away and would guarantee pitch-black darkness.

Jumping into my truck, Chad immediately plugged it in and flipped the spotlight on, turning the deep dark night into instant day whereever he chose to point it. The ride to the cemetery was non-eventful but as we were returning, Chad pointed the light into a deserted old house, engulfed in summertime foliage, that is located adjacent to the cemetery.

Chad screamed out, "What the ...slow down, back-up, back-up!"

I was already creeping along at about 5 miles an hour and could not imagine what he had spotted. Chad looked at me as if he had seen a ghost and indeed that is exactly what he claimed he had seen!

Seconds later, Chad explained: "Just as we came up to the house, I directed the light onto the front porch and there stood an old lady in the hallway of the home facing towards me. I didn't take the light off of her, I saw her very plain."

He continued, "She was wearing a full length dress, sort of torn and uneven at the bottom, her hair was past her shoulders and real ratty looking. Her arms lay limp against her side and she had on no shoes. I could see past her and into the house. I saw an old potbelly stove and a door in the hallway standing open."

When we got back to my house, I asked him to sketch exactly what he had seen. As he sketched, I noticed he had put no eyes, nose or mouth on the subject. When asked about this Chad simply said, "She was faceless!"

The next morning, around 11:00 a.m., Chad, his brother Kevin and I went back to the house to inspect it. I first took a measurement from the road where Chad was the evening before up to the front porch. The distance was 30 feet. Since the female figure he claimed to see was standing inside the doorway with the front door wide open, another 10-foot distance was estimated and added to the 30 feet.

We approached the screened-in porch and found the door locked tight. It was covered with spider webs, which were anchored on an adjoining window frame. Gazing into the front door was a small vine that had grown through the porch, up around the door knob and extended up to the porch light. This was proof to me that no human had used this entrance for a long time.

We cut a path to the back to inspect the rear door and found much the same thing. The rear door was also locked tight. Spiderwebs and vines found there again proved no recent entry had been made. Further inspection of windows around the structure were all but grown over and revealed no broken glass or trampled down foliage. If someone, or something, was in the house the night before --- it was still there!

Things turned even stranger, on Sunday, July 20. I again drove past the house, only this time a middle-aged man was out front cutting back the over-grown foliage. I introduced myself and he in turn stated his name as Mr. White. I then asked him if he was the owner. He stated that he was not, that in fact someone else up the road owns the property. I asked him if he knew anything of the history of the house or who once lived there.

White replied: "Oh yes I knew the folks well. Old man Ball and his wife lived here most all their lives. Mr. Ball died long before Mrs. Ball. Then Mrs. Ball passed away about 10 years ago."

I asked him where did she die and what did she look like?

He said: "She died right here in the house and so did Mr. Ball. Mrs. Ball stayed inside the house long after Mr. Ball passed away. She was a frail looking woman, about 5'5", with straight hair about shoulder length. I always saw her wearing pretty dresses but never wore shoes, she hated shoes."

I then told him of the sighting Chad Gillenwater had experienced just days earlier and told him of the potbelly stove and doorway down the hall that was standing open.

At first, Mr. White was shaking his head. "No, there's no potbelly stove in the kitchen..." he started and then said," hey, you know, years ago Mrs. Ball did have a potbelly stove in the kitchen and that door he saw standing open would have been the door to her bedroom."

White went on to add that, "the house was gutted years ago, even the old solid oak doors inside were removed. So, he couldn't have seen a potbelly stove or even an interior door."

Yet Chad claimed to have seen exactly what the man reported was once in the house -- even though it apparently no longer existed.

A couple of nights later, on July 22, five us (Chad, Kevin, their mother Bev, my friend Tammy and I) were sitting around a campfire and decided to walk over to the old Ball house. The half-mile walk to the house was non-eventful but upon reaching the house, shaky nerves were very apparent. Kevin, Bev and Tammy would not get within 50 feet of the house. A lone coyote started a haunting howl, and then another howling was heard from the other side of the road and seemed very close. Tammy and Bev insisted we head back. As we turned up the hill to our house, the streetlight flickered and then went completely out as soon as we were under it. The howling seemed to intensify. We were now walking very fast and were turning into our yard just as the streetlight came back on without any further flickering. A moment later, the howling abruptly stopped.

The following morning, around 11:00 a.m., I again passed the Ball house and saw a different man cutting down weeds around the front fence. I again stopped and asked him if he was the owner. He stated he was not the owner but quickly added he really didn't know anything about the place. He dropped a large weed he had cut, turned to his black pick-up truck, got in and drove off. The man looked a lot like the other man I had seen two days earlier except for the fact he was much older, a little heavier and not nearly as friendly.

Before and since these most confusing, odd and seemingly meaningless events took place, I have --- and had driven by ---- the Ball house literally hundreds of times. Before Chad saw the mysterious woman, I had never seen a soul at the house. I have not seen one since.

## Ball House Case Summary

Chad Gillenwater was 16 years-old at the time of his sighting, a good student and church-going Baptist. I had known him for two years and during that time, Chad had never once mentioned the old dilapidated house we came to know as the Ball residence, let alone told stories of it possibly being haunted. That evening's activities, before the encounter, were not of ghost tales or haunted lore. It was a simple evening of relaxed interest and general chat.

When Chad first spotted the figure in the house, no gasp or drama was noted, although a surprised look and questions of confusion were noted. He originally believed someone "real" was living in the house, then quickly concluded that was doubtful. Little interest truly existed in Chad's pursuit of the story or the telling of it. The sketch he made was at my request. When I asked Chad how long he had actually witnessed the image, he stated "about a minute". I was there and the fact is that Chad could not have seen the apparition for greater than 8 to 12 seconds. This "extended time claimed" (E.T.C. Syndrome) is a factor found in most paranormal cases. The E.T.C. Syndrome transforms the witnesses' time comprehension to an extended or exaggerated length during the encounter. (See my book *Strange Highways* for a lengthy discussion of his phenomenon)

What does raise questions here is Chad's claim of seeing a female entity, which he described in detail, that matched the description given by Mr. White almost word for word. Chad's remark about her shoeless feet and White's adding that important and odd notation as well raises even more questions! Chad also claimed to see a potbelly stove in the kitchen and Mr. White confirmed its past existence. He also noted that he saw the woman's bedroom door open and White pointed out the room beyond had in fact been a bedroom. This had to be more than a coincidence.

The aftermath was even stranger and have to be added in. I had previously driven by the Ball house scores of times and never saw a soul there. Then, within 48 hours after Chad's sighting, two men on two occasions were outside, both claiming to be cutting weeds and both looking stranger than the last. While seemingly cutting weeds (at an abandoned house), both of them really only seemed to be there for one purpose --- to verify what Chad had seen in the house.

Furthermore, it seemed very strange to me that, first, a polite, unknown, never-before-seen man in a white pick-up truck would be conveniently at the location as I passed and then, a day later, another unknown man, looking similar, but much older, would be there cutting down a single weed by the fence. The second man was not willing to talk much, actually being rude in fact, and then he got into a black truck and drove away immediately after I passed --- almost as if he had been waiting for me.

With a little bit of research I found and spoke with the current owners of the Ball property. They confirmed the details of Mrs. Ball's appearance and then stated that no one should have been at the house doing any kind of work and certainly not cutting weeds. I asked them for, and received access, to the property to further investigate the strange occurrences.

In June of 2004 an associate from the East Tennessee Paranormal Society met me at the location and for the next six hours we took readings and photographs of the house. We found one very "cold spot" in the structure between the front door entrance and the bedroom (this was the location Chad claimed to have seen the apparition). Oddly, in the empty kitchen next to the sink we found a saucer sitting alone on the counter. The saucer from the Edwin M. Knowles China Company (*) was extremely clean and in mint condition. I took it with me as a memento.

Further follow-up (September 2005): Now over a year since the last on site investigation, I went along with Bill Spears, a local research colleague, and again sought and received access to the Ball home. What we found amazed us --- another tea saucer, identical to the last one found, was sitting exactly in the same dust layered, fly infested location as the last. This one again in pristine condition. What, this saucer find has to do with the event

(*) The Edwin M. Knowles Company was established in Chester, West Virginia, but moved to Newell, West Virginia in 1900. In 1963, Robert Boyce and a Mr. Tuck, area businessmen, bought the Knowles real estate.

only adds to the mystery. Although I don't understand it, I can't assume it's a prank. Antique plates such as these have monetary value and are not easy to come by. Did a ghost use these tea saucers or leave them for the investigators to find? And if so, why?

*Did a ghost leave us this antique saucer?*

## The Initiation

In 1958, our family, the Coleman's moved into the house that became our home, 1564 W. Hunt Street, Decatur, Illinois. I still remember the phone number 22360 ---- yep that was it, those were the days before prefixes and cell phones. It was before the common folk had color and cable television, central air and microwave ovens, a simpler time before soccer moms and organized summer activities. Kids had to fend for themselves, fill their summer days with neighborhood togetherness, like baseball games in their own backyards and swimming in a friend's horse water trogh that had been converted into a pool.

Lucky for me, I had a block full of boys about my age as constant companions. There were the Nichol's kids, the Johnny kids, Reed and his cousins and the Carter boys. On that small, dead-end block there lived as many as as eight to ten guys to hang out with at any given time. I have spoken of this group before, a band of boys that called ourselves, "The Rogues of Night". It was not thought of as a gang but a club and every club needed an initiation. The "Rogues of the Night" we were no different.

Our initiations ranged from smoking a corn-cob pipe behind the club house to taping a firecracker to a cigarette and laying it on the windowsill of the "enemy" (the kids on the next street over). This method then gave the one who placed the cigarette on the window a good two minutes to make their escape before the blast.

However, one initiation that no one would do was to knock on the door of old man Kufner. Kufner was a solitary old man who lived in a broken down house in the overgrown field just past the end of our dead-end street. Adjacent to the Kufner acres was, and is, the large graveyard known as Graceland Cemetery. His shack had no electrical power and no phone lines went to the building. Kufner owned no car and was never seen off his property. We imagined that he must have savagely eaten his own cows or scavenged through the neighborhood garbage cans at night. He never he had company and the rumor was that he hated kids! It was said he liked to spy on all of us, quietly sneaking on his belly through the tall weeds and if he could get one alone he would cut off their ears and fingers and toes and feed the pieces to his chickens. No, not one kid wanted any part of that!

Our main clubhouse was located at the end of the street in the rear yard of the Nichol's home. We would often climb on the roof of the clubhouse, bringing the telescope up with us, and spy on Kufner's house across the field. Late at night, we would often see his silhouette carrying an old-time kerosene lantern back and forth from window to window. Then, without warning, he would emerge from his back door and we would scramble down off the roof in terror.

The oddest thing about the Kufner property was the old World War II Avenger airplane that rested wingless, hidden in the overgrown weeds about 50 yards from his back door. That would be my initiation (dare) ---- to sit in the cockpit of the airplane. Scared out of my mind, yet not showing it, I accepted the challenge but double-dared Mark Nichols to join me. One summer evening at sunset, Mark and I slowly and deliberately crept over toward the airplane as the other kids watched from our clubhouse roof.

We stopped about mid-field to confirm Kufner was in the house. If we saw no lantern, it was agreed we would turn back  so as to not chance a Kufner ambush. Ten or so minutes had passed, only hearing the other kids on the roof "whisper-yelling" for us to hurry up as we in turn yelled back for them to shut up.

We crept through the weeds and then there it was, the lantern being carried past a window. Immediately, Mark and I jumped up and ran to the plane. I jumped into the cockpit as Mark kept an eye on the shack. Mark started whispering, "Come on, you did it, lets go!"

I ignored him though. "Gosh, this is so cool," I said to him, "get up here, look, it's really cool."

At that point in my life, I had never even touched a real plane and this was as good as, or better, than sitting in a carnival ride anticipating the thrills to come. I was so enthralled that I didn't notice when Mark left or that five miuntes had passed. Only a couple of flashlight blinks from the shed brought me back to reality. I looked for Mark but only saw old man Kufner. He was about 20 yards away and coming in my direction!

Frightened out of my mind, I leaped from the cockpit and with gazelle-like speed soon found myself in the safety of the clubhouse. The boys later told me that Kufner walked on to the airplane, waving his arm, and then disappeared.

Thinking back today, I wonder about the strangeness of old man Kufner. Looking back on those days, I realize that no parent ever spoke of Kufner and never told us to stay out of his field or ever even acknowledged his existence. The parents would talk about a neighbor's new car or tell us kids to stay out of old man Odem's garden. They would chat about the odd quiet couple at the end of the street or go on and on about Mrs. Sullivan trimming her hedges in her bra once a week -- but I can never recall them speaking of Mr. Kufner.

*Pictured is a plane similar to the one in the Kufner lot. Some readers might recall the disappearance of the 5 Avengers in the Bermuda Triangle. (WWII Avenger; photo courtesy Greg Witmer, Captain Video Productions)*

Another day that I recall found us going down to the field to ride our bikes on the trails at the wooded edge. Almost immediately ,we all noticed large, square holes that had been dug into the earth and equally spaced out. The holes were about 4 feet long, 2 feet wide, four feet deep and some 20 feet apart. They extended the length of Kufner's field.

Unable to ride the trails, we returned to the clubhouse to discuss this latest discovery. One of the kids, I cannot remember who, said they were our graves. He claimed to have counted 10 of them in the field. Another boy thought they were unfinished "kid-traps" that Kufner was building and another thought the holes were for a large fence that would keep us off his land. Whatever the reason for the holes, none of them were acceptable to us and a plan was made to raid the holes that night and fill them all back in! We agreed to meet back at the clubhouse after dark and correct this wrong that had been committed.

I finished dinner, did my chores and rushed out of the house to meet up with the others. As Kenny, Mark, Rick and I waited and waited, no other kids joined us. We split up and went to the other's houses to find out what the delay was. Mark's brothers claimed they were sick, the Johnny kids said their mother would not let them come out (that was a first) and the Carter boys wanted to watch *Bonanza*. Therefore, it looked like the "secret mission" the entire neighborhood band of boys knew about was left up to only us four 'Rogues of Night'.

Making a plan, we decided that two of us would shovel the dirt in as the other two stood watch, switching duties with every other hole. Grabbing our small shovels and wearing dark clothes, the clandestine mission was underway. The first hole was filled in rather fast and we quietly went on to the next.

We had that hole filled in about halfway when suddenly, old man Kufner sprang up from the weeds and began flashing a bright light in our direction! We were immediately blinded and were running and screaming in all directions. We bumped into trees, fell down and one of the kids fell into one of the open holes. We managed to make it to the clubhouse about 10 minutes later, panting and sweating like racehorses. Our shovels had been left behind. One kid had a raspberry the size of a golf ball on his forehead and another had twisted his ankle. Scared and concerned, we all said little and simply went home that night.

Early the next morning found us gathering at the clubhouse as usual. Two kids came screaming up on their bikes yelling, "You guys did it, I can't believe it! Ya did it!"

Dumbfounded we said, "Did what?"

They replied, "You guys actually filled in all the holes!"

Not saying a word, we all lunged for our bikes and whipped over to the trails. Sure enough, all of the holes were filled in perfectly. In fact, we could not even tell where some of them had been. The four of us who had taken on the mission did not say much. We just looked at each other and let the others continue to believe we had filled them all in the night before.

To this day though, I don't know what all of that was about. Why were the holes there? Why did Kufner sneak up on us and flash the blinding light in our faces? And why did he, or someone else, fill the holes all in over night?

The mysteries of Kufner and his ways were far from over. As we all got a little older and some reasoning was attempted, things never seemed to add up. Kufner did not have a street address or garbage collection service and he was never seen at the local grocery stores. Late at night, well past dark, you could see his shadowy figure out walking his old overgrown pasture and continuing on his walk to the cemetery. I saw him many times but never recall seeing him during the daylight hours. He always was dressed in bib overalls, his light brown, unkempt hair never seemed to change and not once do I recall ever hearing him say a word, not even calling to his chickens as most people did.

Time passed. I got a job, a girlfriend and a car but driving by Kufner's, as I headed home on many late evenings, an occasional sighting still manifested (real or unreal?) of that kerosene lantern's flicker from window to window in the old shack.

Then one day, like a snap of your fingers, the old wooden shack was gone, the airplane was moved three blocks away and placed in someone's front yard and the field was graded and a ball diamond was built east of the old Kufner shack. I had heard the entire farm was now the cemetery's property. Curious, I went over to talk to the cemetery people to find out something about Kufner.

Had he died? Did he move? What happened to him?

In 1969, I walked into the office of Graceland Cemetery in Decatur, Illinois on Route 48 to inquire about the disposition of Mr. Kufner and his property. A man greeted me at the door, listened intently to my inquiry of Kufner then frowned and said, "No, no one lived in that shack, the cemetery has owned that land for years".

The office manager looked at the elderly receptionist for confirmation and with that the woman matter of fact stated, "That land has been unoccupied since I have been here and it's going on 15 years now."

The manager continued: "We now need to expand and had to clear the land but wanted to give something back to the neighborhood so we built the baseball field. Is this Mr. Kufner a relative?"

Given my young age at the time, I took a deep breath and saidthat he wasn't but left the office scratching my head, too dumbfounded to fully answer or explain.

More recently, I looked into Graceland Cemetery's history and found that a group of executives from Decatur and Niantic, Illinois originally instituted Graceland Cemetery in 1919. In 1946, a Veteran's section was put in place. In 1950, two 105-millimeter howitzers were acquired for the Veterans section. In 1953, a white marble statue depicting Christ was placed in the cemetery. In 1956, Section R [far west section] was opened and in addition, in September of 1969, the Star of Hope Mausoleum was completed. Land records, cemetery history and even the local businesses had no information about a Mr. Kufner.

So, in another non-conclusive investigation, Graceland Cemetery's own history and staff leaves little room for Kufner to have been there (I won't say lived there) on the "back acres" of the cemetery. Yet from what I know and saw, Kufner was there, and was seen often, from 1958 to 1968! However, was Kufner actually his name? Was he a ghost and does he still walk the old pasture? Was he one of the original (now dead) businessmen, perhaps a lost soul waiting for someone? Was he the guardian of the land that once was a thriving farm? Adding this fact, no less than 10 children could attest to Kufner's existence and four of them could swear they saw him up close! So what or who was Kufner?

I include this story here as an example for today's youth and to put a smile on those of my generation. Those childhood days of the fifties and sixties in a growing Midwest farm town found few activities for kids. It was time and place where imagination ruled, assumptions became fact and dares were something to accept as a badge of bravery or decline as a chicken and be labeled accordingly. Did Kufner savagely eat cows and hate kids? I doubt it. Was Kufner a ghost or more likely a fellow that quietly led a simple life and kept a low profile in a broken down shack? Maybe.... Perhaps Kufner lived off the land or took late evening strolls into town, or maybe even grabbed a cab at the small neighborhood market or hopped on a bicycle that he kept unseen and secure in the shack he called home. Just as likely Kufner was a disabled war veteran or hermit, unable or unwilling to fit into the system. Perhaps he could not speak or more likely, we never gave him the opportunity. In retrospect, I regret running away wildly that initiation night when I was in the cockpit of the old airplane. Who knows? Would Kufner had told me the history of the plane and his personal adventures?

I"ll never know --- but I do know that just about everything that we thought we know about "old man Kufner" was based on assumption. True stories such as this are prime examples of how local legends and folktales may have evolved.

## *Night Marchers of Oahu*

In the winter of 1986, I was fortunate enough to go to Hawaii for a much-needed retreat. Nevertheless, as always, the paranormal hold on me would not allow a simple vacation of lying on the beach or limiting myself to helicopter rides. For me there exists a quest for the unusual, a drive to question the improbable and a need to search out the unbelievable.

This need led me to the island of Oahu, and to the back roads and sand cemeteries of the countryside. It was here I met an old woman who called herself Kilewie Koneli. I told Kilewie of my interest in the local folklore and unusual stories of the islands. In turn, Kilewie told me of the "Royal Walkers", which others have called "Night Marchers". These ghostly silhouettes, which glisten in human form on moonlit nights, appear to be carrying dim burning torches and are seen walking the same paths to temples and healing stones her ancestor's had traveled in the ancient times. Many believe they are the personal guards of King Kamehameha the Great.

As Kilewie and I walked the wide path, the hair on the back of my neck and arms stood on end. I imagined the Royal Walkers to be nothing more than fiction as she spoke but then Kilewie started speaking in her native tongue then abruptly dropped to her knees. After a few long seconds, she stood and explained the tight bend in the path ahead was where she had seen the Royal Walkers as a child. She added, "I always stop at this location for respect and a prayer, it is said to ignore or disrespect their path is dangerous."

"Dangerous how?" I asked.

She quickly replied, "I don't wish to find out!"

Before you hardcore skeptics sum this up as just another tall tale for the tourists, be informed, it was in a small roadside store where Kilewie and I crossed paths, well off the sightseeing routes. Although, I did offer payment, Kilewie flatly refused. Instead, it was she who gave me a gift of a carved Tiki God.

Nothing was seen that evening I spent with Kilewie although, plenty was felt!

# 3. SEARCH FOR THE MYSTERIOUS BLACK PANTHER

Too many sighting from too many places with, at times, physical evidence to support the sightings, warrants this next statement --- Mysterious Cats are out there to be found! The question we need to address is what is it exactly that people are seeing? What is it that's being reported that often leaves tracks and fresh kills in its wake? What truly are these elusive encounters often termed "Black Panthers"?

Most other legendary critters experience more extreme difficulties than the Mysterious Black Panther when it comes to obvious misidentifications, hoaxes, pranks, legend tales, reluctant witnesses, copycat reports and possible exaggerations. At times, other hidden animals vary widely from size, form, color, footprints, actions and interactions with humans but this is not the case with the Mysterious Black Panther. This cat is reported with uncanny consistency; including how it walks, leaps, looks, acts, its size and its color.

Again, I ask if the accepted percentage of true unexplainable sightings is even as low as half of one percent, then what large dark cats are people seeing? Rogue mountain lions? Dark pumas? Escaped panthers? Hybrids? A unique species of some kind? This question has been asked numerous times with as many different answers and it must be asked again and again with each encounter. Investigating each case individually, never to assume a single theory but to prove each case one case at a time will someday unlock this riddle.

Seeking answers to the question of Mystery Cats, when put to some officials, has one unyielding theme and that being that the researcher will receive minimal cooperation, curious understanding and often times, little interest. Many reasons have created this archetype from total disbelief to an unwillingness to physically search an area. Although, I am of the opinion deeper-rooted explanations exist for this often noticed total lack of interest from many of our officials and scholars.

At the top of every Cryptozoological list of obstacles must be the vast number of obvious misidentifications. The researcher might find a score of initially promising, reliable and valid reports worthy of investigation but soon finds the claimed panther-like critter most likely is a seldom seen animal like a bobcat or black coyote.

*(Left) Black Coyote, owner Farris Sensabaugh*
*(photo by Justin Sensabaugh)*
*(Right) Side view of Black Coyote (photo by Justin Sensabaugh)*

Many people have heard the stories or seen the cats themselves but it does not strike them as that unusual. These witnesses must be sought out. Some may even be total non-believers of a mountain lion in, or near, a major Midwestern, Eastern or Southern United States metropolitan area and simply refuse to report the sighting. However, others that have had an apparent large cat sighting show little interest and don't appear to comprehend the significance of a 'black panther' encounter.

Then, the color black itself presents another problem, where the often repeated black color may indeed be a dark brown. Those who see it label it as black when quite possibly a dawn or dusk encounter of a tawny cat may appear black, just as an animal seen at the edge of a shady forest line would appear black. In the bright mid-day sun the "back light" can cause the illusion of black, just like when a bird in flight has the sun behind it.

My investigation for the "Black Panther" holds the theories at bay and considers every possibility on a case by case basis. This kind of hands-on investigating consists of personal interviews, physically checking out locations of the sightings and combing the fields and woods hoping to acquire solid evidence rather than another armchair theory. I belive this animal exists and that not all American Black Panther sightings are misidentified reports of house cats, coyotes and dogs and far from all of them are escaped or released large cats. Furthermore, its extremely doubtful that hoaxes, pranks or total fabrications of large cat sightings have many, if any, foundations in this mystery search.

## The Evidence

In this section, I will only remark on my personally gathered evidence. This is evidence that I know to be true and correct and in many cases, one will find it is in line with other respected investigators.

I have interviewed over 400 witnesses of large dark cat encounters from 1980 to present, from Green Bay, Wisconsin to Atlanta, Georgia and have found strikingly similar testimony in scores of them. First, it is notable that that approximately 75% of our witnesses of dark cats see a large, totally black cat where the other 25% of the witness testimony varies from dark colored to having a white streak or patch. Next, 95% of them describe the cat as having a long swooping tail, powerful hind legs, the distinctive cat-like stroll and piercing eyes.

Interviews of officials, (once they are convinced I am serious and discreet) render interesting opinions and or facts, such as: One game warden admitted, "I'm sure these large cats are out there." Then a Tennessee State Park Biologist told me: "Off the official record, I seriously believe these large cats have small breeding populations in the Smoky Mountains." Plus, numerous police officers from state and local departments have privately told me in one form or another that "We take most all the cougar-type sightings seriously but maintain a public code of silence about it for obvious reasons." Of course, the top obvious reasons are copycat reports, possible public panic and "free-lance" cat hunters.

Then we have the testimony. As stated above, this cat-mystery holds an uncanny likeness not found in other cryptids from one report to the next as to its description, action, photographic and sketch records. Also note, no monetary gain has ever come from a dark-colored puma sighting, no fame and seldom little interest exists save for a few devoted researchers. Regardless, the reports continue to be found, filed and investigated. From Alabama, Illinois, Michigan, South Carolina, Pennsylvania to Iowa, with scores of points in between, these reported large dark-colored, puma-like cats are reported year after year. Sightings occur where no large cats have freely roamed for 100 years, the experts claim, and yet they are not only encountered but also at times even photographed.

People who claim to see a large dark cat use numerous names for the critter and at times, one of the following may be heard ---- Eastern cougars, mountain lions, pumas, painter's jaguarundis, onzas, escaped or released big cats and more often than not "Black Panthers". To put it into perspective, the majority of these sightings are undeniably unknown, hence, they are mysterious cats. Large melanistic (black) puma-like creatures seem to thrive and maneuver, undetected at will in the wilds of the Eastern and Midwestern United States. This is a logical conclusion, even if considering only the abundant volume of narratives.

## *Emory, Virginia*

On August 14, 2003, I received reports of a black puma-like cat that was seen and heard in and around Emory, Virginia. I departed for the location at 6:00 p.m. on August 15 and arrived at 7:20 p.m. immediately speaking with Lee Harding. Mr. Harding lives in the first house as you enter town and was outside on his riding mower. Politely, he stopped mowing and accepted the unscheduled interview. After introducing myself, I asked

Harding if there was any truth to the rumors his town had been experiencing cougar and possibly large black cat sightings.

Without hesitation Harding said, "Yes, as a matter of fact a lot of people around the community have spoke of mountain lions seen recently." When he was asked who, when and where? Harding mentioned he did not have the answers but "a Mr. Foust in town has been keeping right on top of it." Harding continued, "I have not heard any of them being black, although they may be. I have heard many who claim to have heard the screams at night and even some that say they have seen the critter."

After a couple of hours of self-touring the town, trying to track down Mr. Foust for an interview and talking to more locals, my associate and I set up camp outside of the city limits by Hall Creek off of Hillman Highway. This was where the majority of the people we spoke to stated the sightings and sounds emulated from. We had a quick supper, got the coffee going and made plans for a long night ahead.

As evening became dusk and dusk bled into night, we hiked up a dirt road about a half-mile to some dumpsters that we had driven by earlier. Thinking this might be a probable place for our feline to appear,we spent the next four and one-half hours monitoring the site. We tried to stay down wind from the dumpsters, keeping human scent away from them, but this became a task in and of itself as the wind that evening seemed to be changing directions with each passing hour. Although we did see two opossum, three feral (small) cats, one raccoon and a lone dog with a collar, no big cats were seen.

Returning to the camp around 3:00 a.m., we regrouped then walked the banks of the creek. Nothing was seen near this waterway, although the dense foliage and dried branches we stepped on likely would have scared away any local wildlife. Nevertheless, we managed to work our way to a couple of portable deer stands we had strategically placed overlooking the creek by obvious "runs" (trails animals frequently use) earlier that evening and stayed to observe the area for the next two hours. Returning to the camp, it was now about 5:30 a.m., my associate retired as I sat there making notes of the night's events. Within twenty minutes, 6:02 a.m. to be exact, a loud cat-like scream was heard. I froze. My associate came out of the camper and said, "Did you hear that!"

I replied, "Yes, shhhhhhh!"

Again, it screamed moments later. Nothing more was heard but the obvious predator's roar was rewarding enough. The roar/scream may have been from a bobcat, but the piercing sound was exciting nevertheless!

The next morning came and we spent time checking our baited areas and searching trails, paths and runs throughout the woods. By late afternoon, we had returned to town to interview Mr. Foust. Foust, a neighbor advised us, had himself departed to an undisclosed location in search of the big cat. On that note, we returned to camp and again readied ourselves for another long night. Around 2:20 in the early morning hours, the cat was heard again but this time, it was in the approximate area of a bait station and trip camera placement. This gave us hope but the cat wasn't meant to be caught on film during this trip.

As we broke camp to return to Tennessee, a deputy sheriff we had spoken with two days earlier walked up the trail.

"Mr. Coleman," he told me, "our office received another reported sighting of a cougar last night, southeast of here. Appears three fishermen spied the thing along the bank while trolling."

When asked about the animals color or witnesses names the deputy shook his head. "The state of Virginia has basically accepted that cougars have returned to the area. Now it's up to the people that report these sighting to accept the fact our force is not going to launch a lion safari every time someone sees a shadow with a tail."

Needless to saw, law enforcement has more threatening predators to capture, leaving the documentation of black panthers to the Cryptozoologist.

## Reports Continue:

### Investigator Bill Scott filed this report:

In late September of 2002, sometime before 5:00 p.m. Ronald Rhine, 67 of College Park, Maryland was enjoying a relaxing game of golf with some friends at Mountain Golf Course in southwest Virginia. As Mr. Rhine waited in the golf cart for his turn at the tee, he took in the beautiful warm Virginia fall day. It was then that his eyes caught some movement along the tree line 180 to 200 yards away (golfers are well adapted at judging distance). Mr. Rhine stated, "It was a large black panther-like cat walking slowly parallel to the tree line. The cat turned into the woods and went up the mountain side." He continued, "By the time I whispered to my playing partners to look, the animal had disappeared."

### Additional reports from the Panther Archives:

**Illinois, near Byron:** Large black cougar-sized cat observed for over 5 minutes, strolling along the shoulder of highway 72, late fall of 1995.

**Indiana, by Taswell:** two witnesses see a large black panther drinking from Patoka Lake, spring of 2000.

**Iowa, south of Muscatine:** A farmer and his teenaged son chase a large dark colored puma-like cat across their open field, spring 1998.

**Mississippi, near Meridian:** A woman hears her dog barking loudly, at about 6:00 a.m., looks out the back window and sees what she describes as a "black cat the size of a Lab" walking slowly along the woods. She said, "this animal would look at the window, at our dog barking, swish its long tail, and then continue to walk." She added, "It walked and looked like a cat but was the size of a huge dog. Then it went in the woods."

**Michigan:** "It was solid black, and he was a big boy," said Immel, general manager of Independence Village of White Lake. "I'm talking a 150-

40

pound animal, and I have to tell you he was my Christmas present. He was the most beautiful thing I had ever seen! He was gorgeous. It was right out my window, my manager's window here."

**Michigan:** In the 1980s, at least 100 sightings were reported of a large black cat in western Oakland and eastern Livingston counties. One entrepreneur went so far as to print up T-shirts celebrating the animal as well as bumper stickers with the motto, "I Brake for Panthers."

**Missouri Ozarks:** Large black panther-like cat seen often in the Mark Twain National Forest's southern area, fall and winter of 2001, 2002 and 2003.

**North Carolina:** A woman driving home from work through Pisgah National Park encounters a leaping black panther in the beams of her bright headlights.

**Tennessee, Hawkins County:** Jaguarundi sized, dark brown, fast and loud cat seen and heard on numerous occasions, August and September 2003.

**Tennessee, Hawkins County:** Two witnesses see large dark cat with small light color cat eating garbage by a barn, spring of 2002.

**Virginia, Fort Blackmore:** Large black cat seen by edge of road, spring of 2002.

**Wisconsin, in the surrounding area of Fond du Lac:** Scores of witness's claim and report large cat sightings to local police, fall 2003.

**Virginia, Tazewell county:** Two reports of a black panther seen by Swords Creek, August 2005.

## The Research

In Cryptozoology, the implication of a black panther, phantom cat or unknown feline encounter might be termed a "Mystery Animal", rather than a cryptid. This depends on the researcher and is not worth a debate. A Y-Creature, that is to say, an animal known to science yet the reasons for its location and/or behavior are ambiguous, demands that Mysterious Black Panther research be thoroughly and seriously examined on a case to case basis.

Cougar populations of the western United States are arbitrary added to reports with claims of escaped cats from zoo's and released "pets" by their owners as rebuttals from the media and officials for these Mysterious Cats, thus often ending their search. This researcher has considered, and continues to consider, these factors as well as other documental reasons. First, we should consider the Western cougar population (and the known Florida Panther population) as a source for a number of the sightings. I would also agree that rogue lions expand their territories from time to time. Logic tells us that as the main food supply (deer) grows, so would a cougar population.

Next, we have the escaped animals. Although, this too seems to make sense on the surface, the lack of documentation does not support the numbers. If these large cats are escapees from zoos, circuses or traveling carnivals, a quick and obvious alert would be made public. At the very least, the local police would be notified. Moreover, this lack of verifiable proof of escaped cats is not out there to be found.

The released pet possibility also exists but here again, these numbers cannot comprise large blocks of the sightings.

The number one rationality suggested for these Mysterious Cat encounters, which I agree with, must be misidentification. These sightings can be large house cats in a field without a true reference for size, large black dogs quickly scurrying across a dark street, bobcats, coyotes and wolves slithering into the underbrush and the unexplained shadows that are transformed into large dark cat images. All of these certainly play an enormous role. When scale references are absent and when glimpses constitute the encounter, one must consider the likelihood that the subject sighted, and labeled as a black panther, something that was more likely a house cat, jaguarundi or even a canine critter. This is a "most likely" explanation for many sightings.

With very little research, I was able to develop the likelihood of jaguarundi's in East Tennessee. I learned first that, not all that long ago, at least two pet shops used to sell jaguarundi's to the public as pets. Secondly, during the hey-days of the tobacco fields of the south eastern United States, migrant workers from Mexico most likely brought these animals to the region as pets. Two older farmers that I recently interviewed confirmed this probability.

The graph that follows on the next page, "Mysterious Large Dark Cat Sightings", represents 400 reports from eyewitnesses. It includes only areas of the United States where experts claim big cats no longer range, so even if one would conclude the color black is a total fabrication, the reported cat's location would still demand an investigation.

**Note:** Graph data 1980-2004 includes 400 personally researched and/or interviewed eyewitness reports of dark colored puma-like sized cats from AL, AR, GA, IA, IL, IN, KY, LA, MI, MO, MS, NC, OH, OK, PA, SC, TN, VA, WI, and WV. I along with other associates have individual analyzed the reports and jointly determined and agreed the graph titled, "Mysterious Large Dark Cats" to correctly represent, with a level of scientific certainty, to be a low end of the scale for the source of these encounters as reported.

**Note**: Culbertson, N. 1977. Status and history of the mountain lion in the Great Smoky Mountains National Park. Uplands Field Research Laboratory Research/Resource Management Report No. 15.

In 1977, Culbertson examined the status and history of this species in the park. Twelve sightings were reported for the years 1908-1965 and 31 sightings for the years 1966-1976. Culbertson stated, "The number of lion sightings through the years suggest that the mountain lion may never have actually been extinct in the Great Smoky Mountains area. The lion may have been able to maintain itself in small numbers in the more inaccessible mountainous regions in or around the park. The present lion population could be derived in part from this small reservoir... It is believed that there were three to six mountain lions living in the park in 1975, and other lions were reported to the southeast and northeast of the park as well. Lions were seen most frequently near areas of high deer density."

# Mysterious Large Dark Cat Sightings

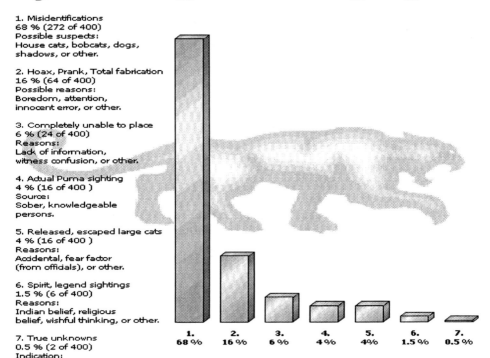

1. Misidentifications
68 % (272 of 400)
Possible suspects:
House cats, bobcats, dogs,
shadows, or other.

2. Hoax, Prank, Total fabrication
16 % (64 of 400)
Possible reasons:
Boredom, attention,
innocent error, or other.

3. Completely unable to place
6 % (24 of 400)
Reasons:
Lack of information,
witness confusion, or other.

4. Actual Puma sighting
4 % (16 of 400 )
Source:
Sober, knowledgeable
persons.

5. Released, escaped large cats
4 % (16 of 400 )
Reasons:
Accidental, fear factor
(from officials), or other.

6. Spirit, legend sightings
1.5 % (6 of 400)
Reasons:
Indian belief, religious
belief, wishful thinking, or other.

7. True unknowns
0.5 % (2 of 400)
Indication:
True possible large dark cat
sightings referred to as Black
Panthers.

| 1. | 2. | 3. | 4. | 5. | 6. | 7. |
| 68 % | 16 % | 6 % | 4% | 4% | 1.5 % | 0.5 % |

**Source Data: Jerry D. Coleman personal files.**

Bar graph design and clip art colorization by Cathy Clark 2004.

# The Cherokee Cougar
## Notes on the Investigation of the Black Puma Mount

This report of a Mysterious Black Cat was originally sent to me by researcher Mike Nimmons and contained within his report were directions to, and testimony of, a mounted large black cat that was found in an Indian owned and operated trading post on the Cherokee Indian Reservation in

Cherokee, North Carolina.

I decided to investigate and departed on Friday, November 2, 2003 from Church Hill, Tennessee. The 140 mile trip was laced with hope but filled with doubt. I've been part of many wild goose chases but if it's even a long-shot gamble, I'm always willing to take a shot.

Upon arriving at the Indian Reservation, my associate and I first located the trading post Nimmons spoke of, called The Chieftain. Pulling up in front of the store, we scanned the wide-open glass front and soon located what appeared to be a black, puma-like cat mount resting high on a shelf towards the rear of the shop. Immediately, we raced back to a local hotel by the Oconaluftee River to set up a base of operation. We double-checked the camera equipment and headed back to the trading post.

Walking into the shop, we noticed two men leisurely seated behind the counter with their feet propped. After strolling around the vast number of mounted animals and reading their individual descriptions, (the black cat's description read, "Large Cats that Once Roamed the Great Smokey's"), I walked over to the clerk and asked if I was allowed to take photographs.

The man, Buddy Gass (Cherokee Indian) stated: "It would be fine to pho-tograph the animals, although another fellow that owns some of the mounts usually charges $5 a photograph, so if a tall gentleman walks in, please stop taking pictures."

After a number of photographs were taken, I spoke at some length with Mr. Gass about the feline he referred to at one time or another as a Painter, Cougar, Mountain Lion, Black Panther or Black Puma. Gass told me the black cat was shot in Tennessee by a fellow about 12 years ago but refused to dis-close the hunter's name. Gass went on to say he preferred not to give me the exact location in Tennessee where the animal was taken, but did add it was indeed shot in Tennessee.

"Can you give me at least an idea of the location: East, West, North or Central?" I asked.

Gass, with a smirk, said, "Sure, I'll give you an idea..... it was one of those you just mentioned." After a long pause he added, "But seriously, it was brought down just north of here, so that would be eastern Tennessee, in the Appalachian's." He then strolled off and started messing with some of the stores stock.

It was obvious Gass was noticeably uncomfortable with our extreme interest in the dark cat mount and showed this with his shorter generalized answers. Therefore, while my associate kept Mr. Gass busy I climbed the rear shelf and "snatched" some hairs from the animals' right rear leg.

The next morning I returned to the trading post to further interview Mr. Gass, the presumed owner of the mount. He changed his story almost 180 degrees on this visit, stating, "Oh Jerry, that's just a normal cougar, not even shot and not from around here at all!"

"Where did it come from and how was it killed?"

Gass replied, "Montana, yes Montana .... but ain't sure how it died, we found it dead." Then he said, "Heck ain't no such thing as a Black Mountain Lion, this one I had dyed."

I replied, "Oh you did?"

Gass then added, "Yep, last year I gave 50 bucks to a hair shop in town, they sent a girl over to dyed it, I wanted it blacker but that's how it turned out, brown like you see it."

This was strange since Mike Nimmons reportedthat the black panther had been seen in the shop at least two years earlier.

 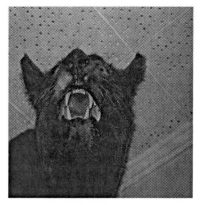

*(Left) Side view of the Cherokee Cougar, the cat is 6' 2" in length*
*(Photo by Tara Coleman 2004)*

*(Right) Cherokee Cougar, note the light colored area*
*( Photo by Nick Coleman 2004)*

With this new claim that the mount had been dyed, and my original thought of the mount being dyed anyway, I had some work cut out for me. I decided to hit every beauty salon in the area. First, I went to the hotel phone book for a list of the area shops and then to city hall for a complete list of salon business permits. I knew that many of beauticians and hair stylists not only work out of their homes but don't bother to get business licenses, so I double checked with each owner I physically visited for additional unauthorized Salon locations. I found that checking out the business permits on the reservation was easier to do than it would have been in an average town. The Indians were very strict about only Indian approved businesses with permits being allowed to operate within the reservation. I still spent an entire day and on this project and no one confirmed Gass' claim of a girl that came over to his shop and dyed any mount.

As time passed and visits to Gass' place continued, I tried to understand, or seek motives for, his story changes. All I could conclude was that Buddy Gass might be in violation of some game law or did not actually own the mount as he had claimed. I then interviewed a number of established taxidermists in east Tennessee and northern North Carolina, showing the photographs of the dark-colored puma to them in hopes they may be able to identify the individual who did the work.

A third generation taxidermist, Todd Godsey in Blountville, Tennessee, with the company name of all things, Bigfoot Taxidermy, stated, "I would only work on a cougar if it was brought in with a Montana tag." Montana came up again. At a couple of the taxidermist's shops that I visited I ran into

Tennessee State game officers checking in deer kills and tags but I had no luck tracking down the origins of the critter in question. However, I did seize the opportunity of my chance encounters and interviewed a state officer.

The State laws in Tennessee and North Carolina are firm --- at no time is a mountain lion to be killed by private citizens. Many assume an open season exists for cougars, but this is absolutely not the case. Furthermore, American Indian's are required to obey the state hunting regulations although, I believe they do not feel the need to abide by these laws. I say this because while on the reservation interviewing individuals, an unspoken birth rite to freely hunt without any restrictions was expressed via verbal hints and winks more than once. Another possible explanation of his story change concerned the fact that Gass alluded to the idea that the "Painter" had religious significant. An old Cherokee Indian legend exists where it was believed large black cats would overlook the tribe as a protector from roofs and rocks that might fall from above.

To the Cherokee Indian, the numbers seven and four are extremely important, as are certain colors. They are consistently mentioned in the myths, legends, and ceremonies of the tribe. The number 4 is representative of the cardinal directions (north, east, south, and west) and the forces (earth, wind, water, and fire). In addition to the four cardinal directions, the Cherokee have three others --- Up (the Upper World), Down (the Lower World) and Center (where we live). (Also 4+3=7 bringing you back to the sacred number 7 again.)

The number 7 represents the seven clans of the Cherokee. The number 7 also denotes the height of purity and sacredness. This level is extremely difficult to obtain with only two creatures obtaining that level in olden times, the owl and the cougar, and this gives them special meaning to the Cherokee. The only other living things to attain this level has been trees, including the cedar (considered the most holy), pine, spruce, holly, and laurel. The owl and the cougar attained the seventh level because they were the only two creatures who stayed awake during the 7 nights of the creation. All other creatures fell asleep.

Traditional Cherokee thus have a special regard for them and honor them. Because they were the only ones to stay, awake they became nocturnal and were gifted with night vision. The cougar is called klandagi by the Cherokee, which means "Lord of the Forest". The Chickasaw called him Koe-Ihto, "Cat of God". To the Cree he was katalgar, "Greatest of Wild Hunters. (*)

This recent finding in North Carolina's Cherokee Indian Reservation hit an early obstacle, which often happens in this field. It appears Mr. Gass is more concerned with his ownership, and /or personal beliefs, than with sharing the straight story. The dark-colored puma obviously has no "papers or tags" to support any legal hunt, or at least none that I have been made privy to. The story changing from a Tennessee kill of 12 years ago to a more recent, death (reasons unknown) of a puma from Montana also adds to the

(*) Legend Source: Deborah Shira

mystery.

Perhaps Mr. Gass has the proper paperwork and does own the puma or perhaps Gass deems the puma an Indian symbol of worship as the legend has revealed. Gass is a strong and proud believer in the Indian ways. During all of the interviews I had with him he continually exhibited a strong and proud Cherokee-oriented theme. Often Mr. Gass would raise an old Indian photograph he kept close to his side and remind me, "This is my Great Grandmother!" At other times, Gass would deviate completely from the conversation and take off on another old Indian tale or tradition.

However, putting aside the changing stories and the side-stepping of direct questions, what we still have here is a very dark brown-colored cat that has been found and documented in a tiny trading post off the beaten path in North Carolina. The cat is 6 foot, 2 inches long and 27 inches tall at the shoulder and may have been witnessed alive somewhere in south-central North America. This cat, which many would swear was black as it leaped into the tall grass during an evening sighting, may have been shot in Tennesee or was Montana road kill --- no one knows or is willing to tell. Either way, the cat does exist.

After my return home, the hair specimens gathered were sent to two universities, where the preliminary results confirmed the hair was one, from a feline and two, not dyed. At the current university involved, East Tennessee State University (ETSU), Dr. Wallace is still examining the hair and conferring with other colleagues.

Below are the most recent e-mails received from Dr. Steven C. Wallace at East Tennessee State University and Christopher A. Whittier, DVM, PhD Candidate from the Mountain Gorilla Veterinary Project.

Jerry,                                                          5/30/2004
Anyway, as for your critter. I have tried my best, but am ready to pass the torch. Unfortunately, like many scientists, there is only so much I can do with a picture and a hair sample. The best analysis would be to see the specimen in person. Don't worry, I am not suggesting that you try to bring the specimen here, but should you end up purchasing it, or want to take a trip to see it some time, just let me know. In the meantime, let's get another opinion.

Hope that all is well,
Steve

Dr. Steven C. WallaceDept. of Physics, Astronomy, and GeologyEast Tennessee State UniversityPO Box 70636Johnson City, TN 37614

Hi Jerry,                                                      6/12/2004
Normally I'd be happy to take a look but I'm actually in Africa- where I work. If you could scan and email photos I'd love to have/see them. I'll be back briefly in October and will send you a note if I can make time to do any analysis.
Chris

Christopher A. Whittier, DVM, PhD CandidateField VeterinarianMountain Gorilla Veterinary Project - BP 105 Ruhengeri, Rwanda, Central Africa

As you can see by these e-mails, science and documentation moves at a snail's pace. However, the study of the Cherokee Cougar is going forward at this writing and additional hair specimen's have been retained and secured in a safe. The secured hair specimens have been secured in the event the mount disappears, as has occurred in similar cases.

Whatever the answer, the search for truth continues and this may be but one piece of the mysterious black panther puzzle. This case of the Cherokee cougar mount is still actively being investigated.

# 4. BIGFOOT'S GALORE! Chasing a Hairy Ghost?

*Sketch by Robert Coppen*

o the not too casual observer of Hominid research it seems that hairy Bigfoot, creatures, a.k.a. Sasquatch, are reported everywhere throughout North America and on just about every other continent for that matter. Does almost every state in the Union and every country on the planet have its own symbolic Abominable Snowman? To suggest thousands of unclassified species and subspecies in the form of hairy bipedal bigfoot-like creatures are living, hiding and breeding directly under our noses in most of the states of America and many of the country's on earth is, to say the least, ridiculous.

Some of the more popular Bigfoot-types are: The Abominable Snowman (Yeti) of the Himalayas, Almas of the Caucasus Mountains of central Asia, Chemosit, which some consider to be Africa's Bigfoot, Chucunaa of northeastern Siberia, Hibagon, which some dub Japan's Sasquatch, Mapinguary, Brazil's own Bigfoot, Maricoxi of South America, the Yowie from Australia and this to name but a few of the more than 37 noted in the Americas, 6 alleged from Europe, 68 hominids of Asia, 24 found on some lists from Africa and 10 mentioned as Australasia. Keeping in mind, none have been captured or confirmed.

This is not an attempt at debunking Bigfoot, on the contrary, but merely to question the vast number of sightings of creatures that have fallen under the heading Bigfoot. I say this with hope that Bigfoot research will soon return to reality. It's doubtful that few people on earth would like to see or know that Sasquatch exists more than I would but should we not be more interested in fact and findings than sensationalized speculation?

The speculation often begins with one solitary shadowy encounter or a few limited and sketchy sightings reported at times in conjunction with a fuzzy photograph produced as solid "evidence". In addition, and as troubling, we are reminded of the biggest breaking Bigfoot news trotted forth in 2004 and 2005:

1. An alleged pair of Bigfoot's captured and contained in Oklahoma awaiting public disclosure via a television special. Hoax!

2. Another person, the third now, coming foreword claiming to have worn a Bigfoot suit in the 1967 Patterson film. Totally unsubstantiated!

3. A fellow testifying on a popular nationally broadcast radio program claiming to have acquired a Bigfoot body then selling the "evidence".Hoax!

4. And more video of Bigfoot absent of verifiable data!

For some, these wild claims, accompanied by flimsy proof, appear to be all that is needed to blindly accept outrageous claims, sending Bigfoot research on the proverbial  runaway train with the gullible as passengers and the hoaxers at the controls. The "Bigfoot Express" temporary gets derailed by legitimate investigators but too quickly steams its way to the next whistle stop of fraud. It is left up to the logical and devoted Cryptozoology researchers and Bigfoot buffs to stay guarded and recognize the "Bigfoot Express", always vigilante and prepared to pull the emergency cord, revealing and ending these scams!

This chapter is devoted to actual Bigfoot research, methods and investigations. No hype, no sensationalism --- in essence a return to reality.

## The Honey Island Swamp Monster

Honey Island's name originated from the first white men that came to the area and noted large numbers of honeybees on a nearby island. The Honey Island bottomland rests between the East Pearl and West Pearl Rivers and the island ranges from three to seven miles wide and 15 to 20 miles long depending on the rainfall. Its geographical location is near Slidell, roughly 40 minutes from New Orleans in Southeast Louisiana.

"This swamp is unique because it's one of the least-altered river swamps in the country. It's pretty much in its original condition, almost a pristine wilderness," says Dr. Paul Wagner, a wetlands ecologist who guides personalized narrated nature tours into the 250-square-mile Honey Island Swamp. Nearly 70,000 acres of it is a permanently-protected wildlife area called the Nature Conservancy's First Louisiana Nature Preserve but the wilderness of the area continues on past the conservation area for many thousands of acres. In this remote area, private residences may be found hidden and scattered throughout the woods and swamps.

The history of the Honey Island Swamp Monster of Louisiana's southern bayou is fairly well known, thanks to a television show called "In Search Of". It was in 1974 that hunters Harlan E. Ford and Billy Mills returned from the inner sanctuaries of the backwater marshland with strange three-toed plaster casts they claimed had been harvested near a dead wild boar with its throat torn open. The two men also alleged that eleven years earlier, in 1963, they had stumbled on identical tracks. They also had an actual encounter with an extremely frightening creature. According to their testimony, the beast stood seven feet tall, was completely covered in grayish hair, and had unmistakable large amber-colored eyes. Heavy rain quickly washed away the 1963 tracks, stated one of the men.

In March/April of 2004, my associate T. S. Christian and I journeyed to investigate and update the area known as Honey Island Swamp and the legend of the monster, a monster the local anglers call the, "Wookie".

Setting up camp in the Fountainbleau State Park by Lake Pontchartrain, we placed a telephone call to the rest of our investigative team. Soon joining us at the campsite were local exotic animal handlers, Rick and Gina Foret. Rick and Gina's knowledge of the southern Louisiana swamps, and their alligator encounters, are well known in many local circles. After a greeting, our meeting put together a simple course of action and the four of us were soon on an airboat racing down to the Pearl River Wildlife Management, better known as Honey Island Swamp. Not only on the agenda was the elusive hairy monster, the Wookie, but we were equally on the alert for the Ivory-billed Woodpecker. (*1)

(*1) At this writing, the search for the Ivory-billed Woodpecker is still underway in the Pearl River Wildlife Management Area in southeastern Louisiana. This is where LSU Student David Kulivan reported seeing a pair at close range in April 1999. Although subsequent searches failed to confirm the initial sighting, Kulivan's report was sufficiently credible, and the area so large and relatively inaccessible, that many think that a systematic, intensive search of the area is imperative.The Ivory-billed Woodpecker was/is North America's largest woodpecker, a striking bird that inhabited southern bottomland forests, favoring old growth. Never common, the bird was last described from the Singer Tract (now Tensas Nat'l Wildlife Refuge) in ne. Louisiana in 1943 and from Florida in the 1950s. The bird also may exist in Cuba, where it was reported in the 1980s. The National Geographic Field Guide to Birds of North America, third Edition says, "Thought now to be extinct in North America..."

Update: On February 11, 2004, a kayaker caught a glimpse of a huge and unusual woodpecker in the Cache River National Wildlife Refuge of Arkansas. The encounter spurred an extensive scientific search for a species that many feared had vanished forever, driven to extinction by the destruction of southern old-growth forests.

The Cornell Lab of Ornithology and The Nature Conservancy led the Big Woods Conservation Partnership in a year-long search for the elusive woodpecker. The team reported multiple fleeting views of the bird, a frame-by-frame analysis of two seconds of video footage, and possible recordings of the woodpecker's distinctive double knock. This evidence has convinced many that at least one ivory-billed woodpecker survives in the Big Woods of Arkansas' Mississippi River Delta.

By the end of the first day, we found ourselves deep in the swamp, where no modern civilization appeared, aside from a few simple shacks on stilts. The abandoned-looking shacks eerily emerged from the moss-draped cypress trees and the larger of the shacks became our base of operations for the expedition. We replaced the for a 12-foot johnboat with a quiet trolling motor for further exploration.

We arose early and as I threw another log on the fire. The 4:00 a.m. cup of cowboy coffee was a welcome stimulus to the damp, foggy wilderness that surrounded us. Unique sounds bounced off the water's surface as I put the day's gear in the johnboat. The shrieks heard were from the blue herons, snowy egrets and white ibis that abounded as the first glimmers of day break filtered throughout the swamp. In no time, Rick and I were trolling where seemingly few had gone before, as we turned into a blind and darkened inlet, a lone, five-foot (*2) alligator glided towards us, curious to our purpose. No sooner had the gator disappeared than a (*3) diamond-backed water snake made its presence known, harmlessly swimming past us.

Hours were spent traversing as far back into the underbrush as was humanly possible. Rick and I then systematically set up a perimeter of trip cameras as we continued to search the water's edge for any unusual tracks. This was the area of the latest Wookie report. We then set up a makeshift campsite and continued to periodically radio the rest of the team at the research shack. Three days and two nights were spent at this location. Although, no Bigfoot-type creatures were seen, heard or even smelled, and the Ivory-billed woodpecker had eluded us as well, I will add this personal observation ---- if something unknown, or thought extinct, does in truth exist, Honey Island Swamp looked like the perfect place to hide.

Returning to the swamps edge, we found the locals were eager to tell

*2. The American alligator (Alligator mississippiensis) is the largest reptile in North America. The first reptiles appeared 300 million years ago and ancestors of the American alligator appeared 160 million years ago. Reptiles are cold-blooded animals, which means their body temperature is regulated by the temperature of the environment around them. This is why alligators are seen basking in the sun, trying to regulate their body temperature. Because alligators are cold-blooded, their body rates are slowed down during the winter months to the point where they can no longer catch food efficiently. For this reason, alligators enter underground holes and remain dormant throughout the winter months.

*3. The diamondback water snake is Louisiana's largest water snake. The record is 63 inches. The average size range usually seen and collected is 3 to 5 feet and very stout. It is found throughout the state of Louisiana. As with most water snakes, it is generally absent from the marsh. Although they inhabit fast moving streams and rivers, they are more common in slow moving waters. Their diet is similar to most other water snakes: they primarily eat fish and frogs. Although the diamondback water snake is a non-venomous species, these and other large water snakes can inflict a very painful bite.

their tales and long time "swamp master", Dr. Wagner told us this about his own encounter. "I was fishing near a canebrake one night," he explained, "and I heard some footsteps. Whatever it was, it sounded big. I turned to see the cane spreading apart and got the hell out of there! Maybe it was Wookie, but I sure didn't hang around to find out!"

Another interesting note worth mentioning, for those of you who are conspiracy theorists, is the fact NASA has a restricted area adjacent to and intermixing in the swamp area. Within two minutes of moseying up the dirt road by the swamp, I passed a government warning sign and security came roaring up in a small white pick-up truck to make sure we immediately departed. The security officers sternly refused my request for an interview.

Wookie reports have been sporadic over the last couple of decades. Most reports are limited to strange sounds that locals familiar with the swamp claim are unusual. However, due to the devastation of hurricane Katrina in 2005, more Wookie encounters are expected to be reported. The reasoning for this will be discussed in a later chapter when discussing "Nature's Natural Force".

*The author while on a 2004 research gathering exploration to Honey Island Swamp. This restricted NASA area is located directly adjacent to the swamp.*

## North American Apes

In this section, we will list the hard evidence that has been collected over the years for the existence of the North American Ape, which some have labeled the "NAPE". The sum total of 40-plus years of following this saga is ---- zero. There is no hard evidence, none at all.

That's correct ---- after over forty years, not only is there no hard evidence for the NAPE, which is claimed to have been seen from Wisconsin to Florida, but if you ask 10 people you'll get 10 different descriptions of this alleged, often-sighted hairy biped.

Some eyewitnesses and researchers label a sighting of an unknown animal they cannot classify immediately as a "Little Bigfoot" or North American Ape, no matter what the description in some cases. They throw about this label sometimes as soon as they hear about the sighting and at other times, years after the encounter. Either way, it's amazing --- amazing that an unknown hairy, elusive creature is labeled, logged and filed as an absolute factual cryptid and many times, those who do the labeling do not even understand the classification!

We also have to keep in mind that many eyewitnesses are young children that could not tell a mongoose from a tapir or adults that admittedly have glimpses at best. The generally accepted description of a Nape is: a chimpanzee-like creature, about 4 feet tall, with no tail, that can walk on 2 or 4 legs, may appear to have green eyes and hide in the bottom lands of mid-America. You can also find this unofficial description of a NAPE; the creature may be dog-like, 3 feet tall, sometimes with a tail, glowing eyes and hide on our city's edge. It can be a shape-shifting werewolf-like creature or even an undiscovered new ape species.

In my book *Strange Highways*, I disclosed an investigation entitled "Hoax Revealed", in that story of a well-documented 1962 NAPE track found in Decatur, Illinois. It was unveiled as nothing more than a prank. Previous claims by a few experts that stated the 1962 print was the best piece of evidence that existed to support the NAPE theory. But don't hold your breath waiting for those "experts" to acknowledge an error or accept the now-documented proof of the hoax! Now available, but never asked for, is a signed and sworn statement from a now 56-year-old man that told the complete story in *Strange Highways* --- a story of just how the now infamous boot-track was made and the hoax perpetrated.

During the summer of 1998, a crypto-minded eyewitness claimed a Nape was seen on his farm near Cincinnati, Ohio. Thankfully, the case did not reach the media because within one week, the alleged "Nape" was spotted again but this time captured and identified as a male black howler monkey. The question remains as to where this monkey came from --- not if it is an undiscovered species.

As for other sightings of apes in the mid-American bottomlands, each case should be individually evaluated, examined and considered for further in-depth investigations.

## The Myakka Ape

On December 22, 2000 a letter signed, "God Bless --- I prefer to remain anonymous" was mailed via the United States Postal Service to the Sarasota Sheriff's Department in Florida.

In the letter, the writer claimed to be an elderly woman who went into her backyard and flashed a couple of photographs at something she heard but could not see. She estimated that the "orangutan" (as it is referred to

54

numerous times in the letter), stood six and half to seven feet tall in a kneeling position. The writer states she did not see the animal until the second camera flash, then "it stood up and started to move."

She was terrified by the encounter, and concerned for her grandchildren's safety, but she baited the area with apples on four occasions to try and get a better look at the creature. According to the writer, the alleged incidents occurred in late September or early October, yet the anonymous letter, void of any exact location to assist the police in the capture of the beast was sent in late December, two months later.

Almost as soon as the case went public, several overly zealous field researcher poorly documented the incident of the "Myakka Skunk Ape" encounter but then have continued to keep public inquiries for a case update at arm's length with a statement of "the case is still under investigation" even though they have barely investigated it at all. It is just this kind of assumption, speculation, sensationalism and lack of any confirmed evidence, or even actual field investigation, that creates the problems for witnesses who sincerely may have, or believe they have, had a true Bigfoot encounter ---- an encounter where evidence, or even the creature itself, might be documented and investigated.

In what became a futile attempt to verify any of the Myakka case as legitimate, I went directly to Florida soon after the case broke and spoke with the Sarasota police, the Humane Society International and the Florida Sanctuary. I also gathered area information on two dissolved animal research programs, as well as interviewed local exotic animal owners and area zoo personnel. None of the dozens of people that I interviewed took this letter or the story as a valid encounter. Furthermore, we then hit the pavement going door to door, for three days, in and around the most likely neighborhoods the letter was believed to have originated from, asking about strange animals or noises and came up empty.

On March 12, 2003 I met with a Tennessee Bureau of Investigation profiler who was kind enough to give the Myakka letter a look. He stated that "the letter has all the ear markings of a hoax, probably perpetrated by bored young college boys."

But are there apes roaming Florida? When seeking the Florida Skunk Ape, or Swamp Ape, one might be wise to first consider the logical alternative to mysterious creatures. Captured escaped or released exotic animals, from monkeys to pythons, that were believed to have been brought in by film companies are documented in Florida and are to this day still being found. This strongly suggests that not only were animals released or escaped but enough animals found freedom in Florida to sustain breeding populations. Unlikely, far-fetched, ridiculous? Not at all. One must weigh production costs, the lack of professional animal handlers, and perhaps most importantly, human nature.

Taking the latter first, human nature is to "give the animal a fighting chance". One must consider the era --- zoo's were nothing more than concrete, steel barred pens in the early days of film and Florida was not nearly as populated as it is today. I would surmise that many animals were released to the Floridian landscape once the crew became attached to the critter. On the subjects of production costs and handlers, obviously one can quickly conclude the high likelihood that releasing the animals or allowing escapes might have been a standard practice.

And there were certainly a number of productions that might have made animal release viable. Today, the crystal clear waters, tropical jungles and thick forests of Florida still serve as locations for the film and TV industries. One of the most popular sites for production has been Silver Springs. Film crews have been attracted to "Florida's Original Tourist Attraction" since 1916 when the silent movie "The Seven Swans," starring Richard Barthelmess and Marguerite Clark, was shot at the park. Many more small films followed, but it wasn't until the '30s and '40s when Johnny Weissmuller starred in six "Tarzan" movies shot at Silver Springs that the attraction's exotic surroundings became a popular location for films.

The six "Tarzan" movies were filmed here, as was the "Sea Hunt" TV series, the horror movie classic "Creature From The Black Lagoon," National Geographic specials, TV commercials...the list goes on and on. There were scores of movies, TV shows and commercials that were shot at Silver Springs and other locations over the years ---- using a variety of exotic creatures. How many may have been left behind?

## Decatur, Arkansas

Cases of hairy bipedal creatures periodically land in the newspapers and on the radio. Of Course, there is no rhyme or reason to the latest or past exposure of these events. Although, when the media does pick up on a sighting, perhaps only to fill a slow news day, interest in the reported encounter usually ends as quickly as it starts. I assure you, many valid encounters never see the papers or hit the airwaves. Their fate is one of being gathered, filed and lost in an amateur Cryptozoologist's notebook or retold as local folktales around campfires.

DECATUR, Ark. Oct. 2, 2003 -- A large ape-like animal has been seen over the last several days in and around Decatur (Benton County) Arkansas. Police Chief Coy Hendrix says he received two calls last week and another call Monday from people reporting that they have seen the animal. The first sighting was on Hill Street in Decatur; the second caller said the animal was headed north toward Crystal Lake, about a quarter-mile away. Monday's caller said the animal was on Benning Road, several miles east of town.

An employee at the Wild Wilderness Drive-Thru Safari in Gentry said no animal matching the description had escaped from the park. The police chief urged anyone with information that could help explain the mystery to call the department. Decatur is about 220 miles northwest of Little Rock.

Following this report from the Associated Press, a news broadcast from the local television station stated that the creature was somewhere in size between a 1 1/2 foot tall brown monkey and a large-sized chimpanzee. No witnesses were interviewed during the broadcast.

Then, 18 days later, and about 500 miles due east, Campbell County, Tennessee erupted with a string of ape sightings.

## The Skunk Ape of Campbell County, Tennessee

On October 20, 2003, news reporter Vince Lennon from WATE, Knoxville 6 wrote:

JACKSBORO (WATE) -- Animal control officers in Campbell County are searching for a primate, perhaps weighing 400 pounds, that's on the loose. And nearly 100 pets are missing.

"I didn't really get a good look at his face because he didn't hang around all that long," Donna Keathley said about when she saw an ape-like creature last week in LaFollette. "But he's big and he's got a really bad stinky odor to him."

LaFollette Animal Control Officer George Moses said, "I believe that the people believe that they see it. I don't have any reason to doubt them, that they're mistaken."

Moses said he hasn't seen the animal but he's certainly heard of it. He started getting calls about it three weeks ago. All the alleged sightings center on the College Hill community, just outside the LaFollette city limits.

Coinciding with the sightings are numerous reports of missing cats and kittens. "All told, over 100" are missing, Moses said.

According to Donna Keathley, when she startled the animal, "This kitten he threw at me, no one knows where it come from."

One College Hill man, who declined to be identified, claims the primate is an orangutan. He said he saw it Tuesday morning leaving stool samples on his property.

Many College Hill residents believe the animal escaped a circus that performed at the nearby National Guard armory a few months back. But the LaFollette Police Department and the Campbell County Sheriff's Department didn't take any reports of a missing animal.

Donna Keathley said her neighbors are ready to shoot the animal. "If I had a gun, I would've shot it."

Then on October 22, Lennon filed a second report:

JACKSBORO (WATE) -- After several residents of College Hill, near LaFollette, said they've seen a loose primate on their property, the sheriff's department has opened an investigation. Residents have theorized that the primate could have escaped or been left behind by a carnival.

So 6 News Tuesday checked on a carnival held at Woodson's Mall in LaFollette in August. The carnival's occupational license was made out for Carousel Amusements. Its owner gave the same answer to 6 News and mall's property manager Mike Orick.

"Michael Parks, who's the owner, told us that wasn't true, that he has never owned a monkey and would never own one. It wasn't part of his permitting for the carnival," Orick said.

Finding a license for the circus held two months ago at the local National Guard armory was more difficult. The last licensed circus wasn't the one that performed there.

Armory officials said they rented the space to Circus Pages of Myakka City, Florida, but the phone number is disconnected.

Campbell County 911 operators said they've taken at least seven calls on the possible primate in the last week.

Capt. Don Farmer with the Campbell County Sheriff's Department said no official investigation was underway until Tuesday because no residents have filed official complaints. "We'll assign an investigator to look forward and a little deeper into this matter."

October 23, 2003
By Vince Lennon - 6 News Reporter

CAMPBELL COUNTY (WATE) -- After seeing reports of primate sightings in Campbell County, a Knoxville Zoo veterinary consultant said he doubts the animal is a skunk ape.

Dr. Ed Ramsey, who teaches at UT, said Thursday he thinks, "...the skunk ape looks like a new world monkey to me. So I'd say if this animal has a six-foot relative out in Campbell County, it would be, I would say, almost impossible to believe. They're typically about 15 to 25 pounds max."

But Ramsey won't totally discount the possibility that the creature is a skunk ape. But he wants more proof before believing it's a skunk ape that's behind a rash of pet deaths.

Pictures of a skunk ape allegedly taken in Sarasota County, Florida three years ago do little for Ramsey and the skunk ape argument. Ramsey also said that monkeys are plant-eaters. If they eat meat it's usually insects and eggs, not cats. Ramsey thinks people are looking in the wrong direction. "If you have an animal that's killing pets, I would actually be more concerned that there's some sort of carnivore that might be out there, a large cat, a mean dog, aggressive dog, pack of dogs, a bear."

LaFollette resident Donna Keathley is one of the few who claim to have seen the creature who's also willing to talk about it. "Tell him if he thinks our story is so bogus, there's a trailer right there for rent. Tell him to come on down and move in with us."

"They can call me what they want to call me," Keathley added. "I know what I saw. I know what I smelt."

Ramsey said UT hasn't received any stool samples to investigate from Campbell County sightings.

I must admit that my method when investigating any such events, including the flap of an ape-like creature in Campbell County, Tennessee, is one of extreme, skeptical caution. I always openly document my findings and constantly review the data to that nothing recorded has been pure conjecture.

With that said, I will present the facts as they unfolded Saturday evening November 22, Sunday the 23rd and into Monday, November 24, 2003.

## TENNESSEE SKUNK APE
**Field Notes --- 26 Nov. 2003**

Shortly after the reports of the ape became public, I traveled to Campbell County, or more specifically Jacksboro and La Follette, Tennessee. Once on the scene, I spent a number of hours touring the town and adjacent areas, becoming familiar with the streets, points of interest and public office locations.

Satisfied with this tour, my associate and I sat up camp between Jacksboro and La Follette. The evening went by without incident and was spent mapping an outline to proceed with in the morning. We awoke early and headed to a local coffee house for breakfast.

The coffee house was where I interviewed the first of many local residents. Every one of the people I spoke to that morning laughed off the Skunk Ape sightings. They had comments such as, "Oh that, it's all bullshit!" or "There's nothing out there but a few crazy people seeing things!"

However, when I went to pay the bill, a fellow came up and whispered for me to meet him outside. When I got to the car he approached me and said, "Something's out there, my Uncle saw it!" The only other information he was willing to give was that the sighting took place two miles south of La Follette.

As I pulled out of the parking lot of the coffee shop, around 10:30 a.m., I noticed that the main road between Jacksboro and La Follette was now peppered with locals selling various goods out of their vehicle trunks as a makeshift swap meet. Stopping at each vendor, pretending to look over their products, I questioned them about the Skunk Ape reports. Not one of them had anything to say more than personal theories.

My associate and I then proceeded northeast on Route 63 to an Exxon station. Here, I fueled up and spoke with a female clerk about the sightings. At first she didn't care to talk about it at all. Then, I asked if the sightings had stopped and she snapped back, "Oh lord no, someone saw it the other day."

I asked where the sighting had taken place.

She replied: "If you turn back around, head through town [La Follette] and turn left at the bank heading out of town, those people in that area reported seeing it a few days ago."

Following the clerk's directions, I headed back southwest. Turning left at the bank (Tennessee Street) as instructed, I noticed a small brown car with a yellow front right fender following me. Going the speed limit, I was soon out of town and in open country with the car still in tow. The car then flashed its lights a few times and I pulled off, but it sped past me and vanished on the road ahead.

Continuing on to a couple of area homes, we walked the grounds and talked about the recent sightings with the residents. They had nothing to tell us but more rumors.

Around 3:45 p.m., I started back to town and up from behind us came what appeared to be the same brown car from earlier in the day. This time it kept flipping its left turn signal on and off as it would flash its headlights frantically. I saw a gravel-like road off to my left ahead of and decided to turn down this road, thinking that perhaps this is what the driver's message was. Apparently I was right because the driver drove by honking, as if his mission had been fulfilled.

Following the gravel road six tenths of a mile, the area came to an open "turn-around" with a creek and woods all around. My associate and I walked some of the area and ventured well back into the woods. Darkness was falling by this time and we felt it best to return to town. We earmarked this area for future exploration in full daylight.

Returning to the main road, I put my left signal on and noticed two white pick-up trucks speeding up the highway with there left turn signals on to enter the single lane gravel road where I was sitting, waiting to make my turn back to the main road. I hurried to make my turn and give them some room because it didn't look like they were going to slow down. Watching in the mirror, and over my left shoulder, the two white pick-ups turned on the gravel road and raced out of sight, almost bumper to bumper. All I could see was one person in each of the vehicles and what looked like some official round emblem on the passenger doors.

Continuing on, a decision I now regret, we went back to town. Our next stop was to Jacksboro and the Sheriff's Department. Here, I was able to interview one of the Deputy Sheriff's. Deputy Starrett was reluctant at first but soon opened up with numerous stories and reports of the Skunk Ape. He stated he had been on most all of the calls as it was his main beat area.

I asked Deputy Starrett about the location for the sightings. "Most of the reports are around or by the caves," he said.

"Most reports are by the caves?"

He replied: "Yes, a number of caves are out there, where this creature has been reported."

I asked him if there were any official reports that I could get of the calls, since they were public record and he quickly said, "Oh yes, many I would think, just call over there (as he pointed to the Sheriff's building) and one of the girls will fix you up tomorrow (Monday).

I asked the Deputy when the last report the Sheriff's office received was and when was the first call? He told me that "the first call was a lady saying an ape had grabbed her kitten and threw it, that's how all of this started and as for recent reports, we haven't had any calls about it [skunk ape] for over a month now."

The deputy also told me of a Jerome Love, who was referred to at the department as a "10-94" (mental case) adding, "Mr. Love owns many exotic animals and has kept this department VERY busy for years."

I also asked the deputy for a standard description of the thing they called the Skunk Ape and he explained that "it's said to be 2 to 3 feet tall, with dark brown or black hair covering its entire body. One gentleman told me he believes the animal has been on his property and wants it taken care of because his grandchildren play there every weekend."

I then asked the Deputy about the alleged shooting of the critter and he replied very sternly that, "no one from this office shot anything, no one even pulled out their weapons. Believe me, if that thing would have been shot by one of us it would have made headline news!"

After wrapping up a few more interviews, I left town and drove back home to Church Hill, Tennessee. On Monday, I started making phone calls. I called the Sheriff's Department first and a dispatcher transferred me over to the records department. Jonathon Wilson in records was quite helpful and stated, "Yes, we have many calls on the Skunk Ape." He then stated he was searching for them on the computer but it appeared no one had entered them, so he said, "Give me about thirty minutes and give me a call back, I'll physically go through the logs by hand and round them up for you."

I waited 45 minutes then called him back. Very surprised, he stated he couldn't find any, "I can't find a one, not one and I know they were here or should be. I started back at the first of October and went through every call."

"Could it be that if no property damage or personal injury was reported then no report would have been made?" I asked him.

"No that's not the case," he replied. "These are disturbance calls I'm searching and not one call is logged, I don't get it!"

This case is far from concluded in my files and remains not only open but active. Now that the "dust has settled", I have since been over to Campbell County a number of times and plan to expand my search for evidence, as well as for witness testimony,  to adjacent county's. At this point though, for all practical purposes, this case has hit an unresolved dead-end.

## *Patti's Sighting: August 1985*

What follows is an encounter told in the eyewitnesse's own words, accompanied by a follow-up interview and case conclusion. This sighting is extremely interesting and comes from what I consider to be a reliable witness.

*As usual, I was out at our cabin near Lynn Lake Manitoba with my Father. The cabin is about 10 miles from town and 3 miles across a lake. Very rugged terrain. It's hard to get to unless you know how.*

*Dad heard via CB radio that company was coming, and asked me to check for a boat. On may way down to the landing, I heard a branch snap and I looked to my left and saw a "something" digging in the dirt. I thought "BEAR!" and froze. I was wrong! The "something" stood up on it's back legs, "shooed" me away with a hand gesture, and in 3-4 steps was back into the deep bush where I couldn't see it. (this all took less than 1 minute)*

*I ran back to camp and said "There's something weird out there!" To that my dad replied "You know they are there."*

*I noticed the head shape (had the crest like a gorilla), a brow ridge, and dark brown eyes. The hair was short and sleek and a reddish brown. It stood a lot taller than I am (I'm 5'4"-5'5") so a good guess is about 7 feet tall. No neck seen, no ears seen. It's hands were not hairy but reminded me of leather gloves. Didn't notice fingernails either (I mostly looked at the face). I didn't notice the typical "bad smell" either.*

*The company came and left without incident I was freaked out and wanted to leave). The next day 2 men came and asked questions and looked around. No cameras, notepads, or other equipment. Found out this spring who called who. The company that visited called game wardens. Don't know if it was them that showed up, as no-one seems to remember any names, except "it was French". Found out some other weird info too, but it doesn't relate to this account.*

*I just realized I forgot some details:*

*Yes it made eye contact. Skin color was a dark brownie-red almost like North American Indian but more ruddy. Facial features were very flat, semi-rounded chin (not squared off), large lips, almost puckered. I assume it was a young female or male because I did not notices breasts. I couldn't even guess a weight, I'm horrible at guessing weight, even my own! About the shooing, have you ever seen old men when they are fed up and go "BAH" and wave/push their hands? Just like that but no noise.*

*It was fully standing at the time also. It turned and walked away after that. Head was down and no arm swing, but long arms, very muscular, but thin build, like it was almost starved or something, or very young? Like a teenager (human) gets--like they've been stretched and not filled out yet. How could I forget about the prominent butt? Yeah it was. Sounds weird but it was up off the ground, whereas a bears would be close to the ground cause they have stubby legs.*

**Interview:**

1. You stated; "On my way down to the landing..."
   Question: How far was the walk to the landing?

   Answer: The walk I'd have to guess, I'm not sure, takes about 5 minutes to walk from the cabin to the landing for a person that's 5'4"

2. You said; ""shooed" me away with a hand gesture.."
   Question: Can you recall, which hand was used or was it both?

   Answer: It used both hands, like a fed up old man that waves kids away?

Question: Did any grunt or heavy breathing accompany the "shoo" gesture?

Answer: No, no noise at all.

3. You said, "my dad replied, 'You know they are there."
Question: What did your dad mean by this?

Answer: I had no idea then.

Question: Did he explain it then or since?

Answer: To make a long story somewhat shorter, I started dating a Bigfoot investigator and found out (through my boyfriend) what he meant. My father had heard stories of bigfoot in that area, but had never seen one.

4. Your statement, "The next day 2 men came and asked questions and looked around.."
Question: Can you describe these individuals or recall any details at all?

Answer: Yes I can, they were both tall, about 6 foot, in blue jeans, t-shirts and "bush" flannel jackets. One had a ball cap on, dark hair for one , short cut, blonde brush cut for the other. What they were wearing, hair cuts, shoes or boots, a vehicle, etc.? Vehicle was a Lund inboard boat. Found out that one man was a game warden.

Question: How long did they stay and who talked to them? Do you recall any of their questions?

Answer: They stayed at camp for about an hour. The only question they asked me is where I saw "the creature"(their words) so I showed them. I assume they talked to my father. I went fishing with friends in the canoe.

5. What was the weather like? Before the encounter and immediately after-wards?

Answer: It was clear and warm for up north! About 20 Celsius. (before and after)

6. Exactly what time of day was it?

Answer: It was after 12pm, closer to 1:00-2:00pm

7. Were you on any medications or similar drugs including but not limited to alcohol? And if so, how long before the sighting was it used?

Answer: Nope, not at all, I was 2 months pregnant though.

8. How much sleep had you had the night before and were you in reasonable good health?

Answer: Good sleep, always in the fresh air! And excellent health.

9. What is your name? Age at the time? Area of your home (at the time)?

Answer: My real name is Patti XXXX, I was 17 at the time, and I lived in Lynn Lake Manitoba, Canada.

10. Before the event: Did you believe in strange phenomena, Bigfoot, or any similar topics? This means avidly, such as a fiction writer, active ghost hunter, fantasy painter, etc.

Answer: I was "into" sci-fi movies, and books, liked the idea of aliens. Didn't really understand about Bigfoot, I thought it was a made up story to scare kids. But no, no I wasn't then.

11. What has changed (if anything) in your life since the occurrence? Dreams, phobia's, a keener sense, depression, etc.

Answer: I've had nightmares off/on about it. But they always change and are never the exact same twice. I'm very careful in the bush now, I watch where I'm going, and what's around me a lot more.

12. In person, by chance --- have you met any other people with very similar stories to tell as yours?

Answer: I've met a few people with Bigfoot sightings, but nothing like mine at all.

13. Do you have a theory about what it was that you saw?
    Answer: I'd swear it was a bigfoot, but I'm not totally sure what a bigfoot is. My first impression is that it was a gorilla. A really tall one.

14. Did you sell this story to anyone or contact the media at the time of the event?
    Answer: Nope, never.

15. If this was to happen again, have you given any thought as to how you may react?

Answer: I'd really like to see another one, just to prove to myself that they are a true animal. I'd probably be really scared, then happy that I had a second chance to see one.

16. Have you been back to the exact location? If so, how often and how recently?

64

Answer: I kept going back there for another 5 years, so up until 1990. Haven't been back to the cabin since but visited Lynn Lake twice since then. Once in 1992, and again in 1995, haven't been back after that.

17. If you wish your real name not be used would you supply a pen name here:

Answer: Patti. Using my first name is fine with me.

**Case Conclusion:**
We will never know what Patti actually experienced that August day in 1985, other than to say "unknown". What is so compelling about this report is her description of the "shooing" gesture and thin stature of the creature. This is unique because it is unlike the typical Bigfoot encounter of a huge, healthy, hairy creature. I find this report to be highly credible.

# *Bigfoot Research, Rumors & Rhetoric*

I've gathered numerous and often repeated Bigfoot rumor's over the years. Few are worth sharing but I'll share some of the more interesting items of circumstantial evidence here on these pages, strictly for the sake of demonstrating the shift in thought. You will not read ridiculous tales of Bigfoot attacks, abductions or rapes of human women, nor will you find unsubstantiated close encounters that involved boulder throwing, tree twisting or overturned camp sites.

Lack of  Bigfoot documentation has given birth to total speculation sends many researchers in the directionof the Internet, which is rife with peronal opinions that are stated as fact and many missed and/or forgotten opportunities. This  has driven our once seriously thought of as flesh and blood, undiscovered, hairy hominoid into a land of fantasy and fraud. Bigfoot has become more of a social and physiological phenomena than an actual cryptid and where the creature was once hunted by well-planned expeditions, it is not pursused from a computer keyboard.

Why has this dramatic turn of events taken place?

The answer is quite obvious --- because many researchers and buffs found Bigfoot long ago. Not the actual creature, oh no. They found Bigfoot to be their meal ticket and their proverbial 15 minutes of fame. One can go to any Bigfoot forum on the Internet or convention and see who is hunting Bigfoot via "Google" and personal opinions. On any given day, one can hear and read outlandish tales, personal encounters, investigative reports and even blatant guesswork portrayed as highly educated statistics and facts by researchers who claim to be Cryptozoologists. The only true link that most of them have to Cryptozoology are the screen names they choose and the basic theories of the field. For many of these people, Bigfoot has paid for airline trips (vacations) that are gobbled up so that they might speak at the same recycled conventions --- where their hallway book stalls and requests for donations far outweigh the value of their lectures.

But not all is lost...

For a multitude of people, who have a legitimate interest in the real, felsh and blood Bigfoot, the creature is not just a means to entertainment or an income. They take pride in logic over assumptions and view Bigfoot research in this new millennium to be, at best, absent and at worst, non-existent. They look for real answers and not Bigfoot as a ghostly, paranormal ape man with astounding supernatural powers to explain his elusiveness. This only serves to pull the curious further into the grasps of fiction. The general public demands, and deserves, better --- but too few crypto researchers are supplying it.

The following story from my colleague Paul Schuman demonstrates a logical deduction to an unknown encounter. Please note that assumptions within his testimony are absent. Paul then further exams some of the possible "issues" with Bigfoot research as a whole.

### Rock Banging in the Sierras
Paul Schuman is an independent, amateur Sasquatch researcher. He has been interested in Sasquatch for over 30 years. He is not a member or affiliated with any research organization. These are his words:

*In my late teens and early twenties, I did a considerable amount of backpacking in my home state of California. Most of the time I would hike in the Sierra Nevada mountains, since we lived in the foothills. I always hiked with at least one other person, not only for safety, but also to share the experience. This is an account of part of one of those backpacking adventures that occurred in 1978.*

*My friend Kevin and I had hiked together many times. Though we were young (I was 18 and he was 16), both of us spent a lot of time in the outdoors backpacking, hunting, and hiking. We knew how to use a compass and a topography map and felt comfortable with our outdoor skills. We made several backpacking trips to an area north of Interstate 80 near Cisco Grove, below the Black Buttes. We had an encounter with a cougar there once, but that's a story for another time.*

*Since we were familiar with the area north of Interstate 80, we decided to check out the area south of the Interstate. Studying our topography maps, we found a trail that looked interesting. The trailhead was at a place called Rainbow. We figured this was a good place to start our exploration of the area.*

*On the morning of the trip, we arrived in Rainbow. There was a parking area at the trailhead where we could leave the car. Now there's something you should know about this area. Interstate 80 follows a valley here, so it's uphill on both sides. Steep uphill. Being young and invincible, we attacked the trail with gusto.*

*After about a mile of uphill switchbacks with full backpacks, the novelty of the hike was wearing thin. After another half mile, we were questioning our sanity. Finally, after about two miles, we reached the top of the ridge and hit a stretch of fairly level trail. We hiked another mile, then stopped to take a break. Even though most of our hike to this point was uphill, we only had another three miles to where we planned to camp and a lot of hours left in the day, so we started thinking about a side excursion. We broke out the topography map and noticed a lake about a mile and a half to the east.*

There were no trails to the lake. This was the perfect excuse to test our orienteering skills.

If you're not familiar with orienteering, it's the art of finding your way where there are no trails. In our case, we decided to use our compass and map to find the lake. It's not really that hard. First you position the map so it's pointing north, using the compass. Then you figure out where you are along the trail, using landmarks as references and the compass to take bearings to the landmarks. Once you figure out where you are, you can figure out the compass heading to get you to where you want to go. Using the compass, look in the direction of the heading and find something like a lone tree or big rock on that heading. Hike to the landmark you picked and find another one. Continue until you reach the place you want to be.

Our skills were sound and we came out on a ridge above the lake. The lake was to our right and there was a basin to our left. The basin was somewhat unusual. It was mostly bare rock, but there was a stand of evergreen trees in the middle. The stand of trees was about fifty feet across and almost perfectly round. Everything else in the basin was bare rock. The basin was about 150 yards across and was surrounded by forest on three sides.

As we stood on the ridge, the trees in the center of the basin began whipping in the wind. There was no wind where we were standing. The trees whipped in the wind for about thirty seconds, then stopped just as abruptly. My first thought was a whirlwind, but the trees surrounding the basin were never disturbed as they probably would have been if a whirlwind had entered and left the basin.

Immediately after the trees stopped blowing, we heard the rocks. There was the distinct sound of rocks banging together. The sound was coming from an area about a hundred feet down slope from the trees in the middle of the basin, about fifty yards from us. We could clearly see the area where the sound was coming from, since everything between us and the sound was bare rock, but there was nothing there that could be banging rocks together. After about thirty seconds, the banging stopped.

Being young and dumb, we decided to check out the source of the sound. We hiked down to the area where the sound was coming from. We found some fist sized stones, which could have made the sound, but nothing bigger than a rabbit could have eluded us. We found a spring flowing out of the ground right where we heard the sound. We searched the area and the stand of trees for any animal that could have been making the noise, but we found nothing. I looked at Kevin and said I think we should leave. He agreed. As we left, we hiked around the lake. We came to a shallow cave. Inside the cave, we found a circle with a cross through it. When we laid the compass down, the cross lined up with the cardinal points of the compass. Strange, but I don't remember anything else from that backpacking trip. I have no idea where we went after that experience.

So, what could have caused these strange events? Some people believe spirits live in the vicinity of springs. Some people say Sasquatch bangs rocks together, while others say Sasquatch can travel between dimensions. Could it be an invisible Sasquatch? Some would say it was the wind. Some would say it was the overactive imagination of a couple of teenagers.

What do I think? I honestly have no idea. It wasn't our imagination, *since we were merely hiking to a lake and the events took us by surprise and we both experienced the same thing. We had only been concentrating on finding the lake and didn't talk of Sasquatch or ghosts or spirits prior to this. I'm a skeptic when it comes to Sasquatch or spirits. Chalk this one up to one more unexplained event along a side road from a strange highway.*

### Thoughts on the State of Sasquatch Research

Growing up in northern California, I first became interested in Sasquatch at age 12. I read every Sasquatch book at our library. I've back-packed, hunted, and hiked all over northern California and have done Sasquatch research in many other places. So far, I haven't had an encounter I couldn't resolve by more mundane explanations. The more research I do, the more convinced I am that Sasquatch doesn't exist. I still hope it does, but the evidence leads me toward nonexistence. So, keep in mind I'm a skeptic as you read on.

**Bigfoot/Sasquatch Organizations:** I have several problems with the way many of these organizations operate. The biggest problem I see is some of them seem to be in it for the money. They didn't start out that way, but appear to have drifted toward the money when they realized there was some to be made. There's a big problem with this. It's in the organization's best interests to keep people believing Sasquatch exists. If you need to keep people believing, at a minimum, you will embellish the evidence in favor of existence, while playing down the evidence against existence. At worst, you might fabricate evidence to keep people paying. Regardless, an organization that makes money from Sasquatch believers can't be objective in their research.

Another problem is just about every Sasquatch research organization keeps their best evidence secret. Of course, there are several reasons for this. One goes back to the money. If someone can prove existence, they stand to make a lot of money. Some estimates are well over a million dollars. Another reason is ego. Most people don't want other people using their hard work to further the other person's research. Finally, most researchers don't want someone coming to their research area and doing their own study. While these organizations have their reasons for not sharing good evidence, in the long run, it negatively impacts the search for Sasquatch. If every organization cooperated and shared information, who knows how far research would advance?

This brings me to my next point. Many organizations disparage other organizations, at least "behind the scenes." If you spend a lot of time online in the various Sasquatch forums, you will see a lot of sniping of one organization by members of another. It's purely an ego thing, but it doesn't advance the cause at all.

There are some benefits from these organizations. Many have sightings databases where you can look up the sightings in your area or the area where you plan to research. The problem is you have no way of knowing the criteria for a report making the database or being rejected. There could be other reports from your area which were rejected because they didn't meet the criteria, but are valid reports. There are others that made the cut, but are obvious hoaxes. I'm sure these organizations do their best to keep out the hoaxes, but some make it through. I'm fairly sure that the absolutely best reports don't make it to the database, at lest not at first. I believe the organizations keep the best reports secret at first, so they can research them privately.

*Independent Researchers:* A lot of what I said about Sasquatch research organizations also applies to many independent researchers. Because there is money to be made, researchers keep their evidence secret. Also, if you spend some time online in the Sasquatch forums, it will amaze you. A group of Sasquatch believers will tear apart any report from some-one they don't know worse than the most ardent skeptic. In my opinion, this causes people who might have something to contribute to withdraw com-pletely. If someone with a good sighting reads what happens to others in these forums, they will probably not report their sighting at all. There is a tactful way to question a sighting report, but it is seldom used.

Another problem with independent researchers is they have to fund their own research. For the most part, this means they can't afford expen-sive DNA testing or the latest thermal imaging devices. Because of money limitations, potential physical evidence never gets properly tested. Someone may have proof of existence in their possession already, but can't afford the tests to prove it.

Finally, the independent researcher usually has a full time job. This lim-its the amount of time they can spend in the field. I'm lucky if I can get six 2-3 day expeditions done in a year. I'm sure most other researchers face the same limitations. Additionally, married researchers have to spend some of their off time doing family things. If, as some have said, Sasquatch needs time to get used to your presence, this isn't going to happen with most researchers.

*Overall:* It always seems like we are "a year or two away" from proving Sasquatch exists. We were a year or two away in 1958, when tracks were found at Bluff Creek. We were a year or two away in 1967, when the Patterson-Gimlin film was shot. Just recently, when footage was aired from Manitoba, some "experts" said we are a year or two away from proof. Yet, somehow, it never happens.

The Internet has been both a boon and a bust for researchers. On the positive side, a researcher can look at thousands of sighting reports and find hundreds of articles in minutes. The latest sightings are sometimes available in hours. On the negative side, hoaxes can also circulate in hours to a broad audience. There's also a less than honest element, who will charge to see their "evidence" on a particular website. If one pays, the evi-dence turns out to be a "blobsquatch," hoax, or something available for free on other sites.

Some say you can't prove Sasquatch exists through DNA analysis with-out a known Sasquatch sample. While this is true, there are tests to deter-mine how close a particular DNA sample comes to known species like humans or great apes. This testing is expensive, but a sample from North America which comes back as close to human and close to great apes, but *different from either would be interesting indeed.*

*If Sasquatch exists, I believe it will be proven by someone finding a body in the woods or a semi-truck hitting and killing one. I honestly think this would have happened by now if they exist. Maybe it has, but if so, it hasn't made the news.*

*To sum up, I don't think the state of Sasquatch research is any better than it was 40 years ago. There are still hoaxes, but they are better and more elaborate due to advances in technology. Egos haven't gotten smaller over the past 40 years, so nobody wants to share their evidence. Then there's the money. If there's one thing that negatively impacts Sasquatch research more than any other, it comes down to that one word... money.*

**by Paul Schuman**

Now that we have at least openly acknowledged this 180 degree phenomenal swing, or "stuck-in-the-mud Bigfoot research", and the issues it has brought about, it might be best to look at some of the recent popularized claims labeled as circumstantial evidence, logical speculation and Bigfoot probability rather than farfetched rumors and pointless agenda-oriented opinions.

### A. Bigfoot & DNA

Recentluy, a sample of alleged Bigfoot scat (droppings) was being sold on the popular Internet auction site, eBay. "Cass", an active researcher of Cryptozoology, purchased the specimen and had it shipped to me for examination. I immediately took it over to a veterinary colleague located in Rogersville, Tennessee. The initial examination revealed this: the host interestingly ate; fish, insects, flowers (possible morning glories), various seeds, egg shells and a small rodent. Further examination by way of DNA analyses confirmed the source to be human.

This brings up an interesting possibility if one dismisses the idea that this might be a hoax, we are left with several possibilities as a source for the droppings, including human, contamination of another type of matter by humans and samples that are part human or perhaps even feral human.

Many specimens of Bigfoot scat allegedly return as inconclusive. However, I have found all specimens I've had examined (more than a dozen to date), or have seen other researchers documentation of tested samples, do return with conclusive results to a certain or multiple species, whether it's a bear, human, dog, raccoon, etc.

The point is that perhaps what we're finding is not at all what we think it is but rather only what we hoped it to be. Consider this, two of the ongoing arguments used to explain the absence of a Bigfoot body are that Bigfoot is intelligent enough to bury their dead or that the forest quickly consumes any evidence of a dead creature. There have also been arguments and opinions that exist stating that Bigfoot is so intelligent that the creatures have been known to cover their tracks and to avoid cameras. Some of them, it's been said, might even be able to speak!

If these theories are to be seriously and logically considered, then how is it  that our intelligent creature Bigfoot poops everywhere on the trail and

70

allows the droppings to be found with ease? Would they not cover it or hide it or know that it would quickly decompose? This leaves little doubt in my mind that in order to get an actual sample of Bigfoot scat, one must be in the right place at the right time, perhaps only minutes behind a Bigfoot.

One high profile case, which occurred at the Carter farm in Tennessee revolves around not only testimony, but DNA specimens of scat and hair. It is one of those cases that refuses to go away. It is a case filled with inconsistencies to the skeptic and the anticipation of a conclusion for the believer. Researcher Will Duncan did collect a specimen that I would suggest might be what so many allude to with questionable conclusions. What follows is Will Duncan's personal statement in reference to the before mentioned specimen:

"In a barn loft in Tennessee, approximately seven feet off the ground, in a closed up and abandoned barn and without a ladder for access, we found what probably amounted to 200 lbs. of roughly human sized scat. Some specimens were collected under clean conditions and submitted to a prominent scientist for analysis. He found dog, bat and human DNA. The bat DNA may have come from bats in the barn, but dogs were very unlikely to have been able to access the loft, and several dead dogs, one skeletonized and hanging in a tree, were found in the vicinity. One wonders whether the source animal perhaps had human DNA, as no other DNA was found. A wildlife rehabilitator suggested to me that a juvenile Sasquatch, perhaps trying to conceal its presence from others, was using the barn loft as a latrine."

This case is still actively being investigated.

## B. Bigfoot Bones

Various tales are told of Bigfoot bones being rushed off to an undisclosed university for study. Under secretive and state of the art examination these bones have been documented to belong to an unknown hominoid. I find this popular and weak so-called evidence to be nothing more than an often repeated rumor without any basis.

It is a fact that few bear carcasses are found in the wild. It is this point that gives some credence to the argument as to why no Bigfoot corpses have been found. But, if the population of Bigfoot is even as high as one-tenth of the bear population, then should we not look as the ration of sightings of Bigfoot vs. bears? If the population of Bigfoot is in the five digits and the black bear is known to be around 750,000 in North America, should Bigfoot-type's be seen as often as they are reported and if so, would not bones be fairly easy to locate?

However, many theories suggest Bigfoot families bury their dead, hence we find no bones. This type of total speculation does not address how the tool-less creature achieves this and seldom suggests the logical use of cadaver dogs or echo devices to locate such burial areas.

If the bones are really out there, then perhaps the best results might come from actually getting out in the field and searching old creek and river beds, as well as hidden caves, rather than dreaming about Bigfoot burial grounds.

### C. Bigfoot Shelters

Again, this is where I run into a major problem with the debate and speculation on Bigfoot shelters. One cannot have it both ways, either Bigfoot is an intelligent, elusive creature or Bigfoot is an average-minded, ape-like creature that builds nests, poorly constructed lean-to's and has been blamed for stealing blankets from clotheslines to lay upon in their caves. The fact is, from my own investigations, research and colleague-shared data, these "shelters" and bedding areas (9 out of 10 times) can be confirmed with little effort as being the work of adventurous young humans who are out making their "secret forts".

On many occasion, I have investigated numerous caves and mine shafts with interesting findings. However, I wouldn't declare any of them to be Bigfoot havens with any certainty. In spite of this, I have found odd items in caves, strange things in mine shafts and oddly formed lean-to's but I have no hard evidence to suggest that these findings were anything other than a homeless person's temporary retreat, a group of local kids' fort or a unique find that we later determined to be an old Civil War soldiers hide out. We have seen and heard about the Indian caves and the bear's dens but still actively seek the Bigfoot lodge. If Bigfoot is real, then the most likely place to look for his shelter would be in natural formations such as caves and in forgotten and abandoned mines.

### D. Bigfoot Lifestyle

Assuming Bigfoot is an undiscovered primate, let us put forth some of the more popular hypothesis.

### What would the longevity of an average Bigfoot be?

Considering the following known species life expectancy in the wild, chimpanzee may live 35 to 40 years, orangutan around 35 years and gorillas have lived 35 to 50 years. It would be safe to deduce that a Bigfoot may live anywhere from 35 to 50 years or perhaps as long as 55 years.

### What would Bigfoot's gestation period be?

Again, taking known data from the great apes, which is 250 to 270 days; this too would be in the ballpark of the Bigfoot's gestation. Another logically assumption would be that a female Bigfoot would give birth every 2 to 4 years, probably closer to the latter.

### What would Bigfoot's main diet be?

Chimpanzees have been observed hunting monkeys and small mammals thus adding to their diets of leaves and fruit. The Gorilla's primary food source is leaves and small shoots and the orangutan's chief food is fruit. Therefore, Bigfoot's diet must largely consist of leaves and young plants, occasionally expanding the diet to different items as what is also found in other primates, such as small mammals, eggs, insects and fish.

### Would Bigfoot communicate, just as other primates communicate?

We should expect Bigfoot to do so quite proficiently.

### Would Bigfoot live in groups?

Other large apes exhibit highly developed aggregation for safety, mating, child rearing and food gathering for survival. It's doubtful that Bigfoot would be any different in this respect.

### Would Bigfoot migrate?

It's doubtful that migrations would take place in the manner of some species of birds and fish but movement and expansion would surely take place due to climate conditions, food sources, mating and safety issues.

### How large of a Bigfoot population might we expect to encounter?

Numerous theories throw out number's ranging from 75 creatures on the absolute verge of extinction to 3,000 destined for extinction to a possible high of 10,000.

In conclusion, Bigfoot's exodus appears inevitable with little chance to survive. With dwindling forests, food supply levels in question, and the hard facts that no Bigfoot body, bones or DNA evidence has surfaced draws the logic to only one undeniable conclusion: Bigfoot is no longer roaming, alive and undetected. The 1967 Patterson film may have been the first and last true vision of this creature we will ever capture even on tape.

However, on the other side of the coin, long before the name Bigfoot was dubbed, or the Ray Wallace accounts of large beastly tracks hit the media or the Patterson filming in Bluff Creek, California debate began, the American Indian legend of Sasquatch existed and testimony from reliable witnesses continue to this day being reported as fact.

Other note worthy items to contemplate are the large inaccessible land masses that still exist in the Sasquatch territories and specimens such as hair, tracks and photographs that are still being found, gathered and examined. Separately, these may be explained away, or found to be trivial, but jointly these items should not dismissed and do require a closer look.

The choice is up to the reader:

1. Bigfoot is not real and never was.
2. Bigfoot is a real undiscovered species.
3. Bigfoot is some unknown paranormal force.
4. Bigfoot is some kind of projected mind image.

5. Bigfoot was once real but now extinct.
6. Bigfoot is/was hoaxes & pranks.
7. Bigfoot is/was real only in legend.
8. Bigfoot is more than one of the above.
9. Bigfoot is none of the above.
10. Bigfoot has me dumbfounded.

I choose number 10, which translates to continuing the research with an open logical mind, weeding out the sensationalism, ignoring the assumptions and properly investigating the events.

# 5. FLIGHT OF THE THUNDERBIRD
## with Cathy Clark

**A**ccount of Thunderbirds have been around for hundreds of years. The stories all tell of huge, unknown flying birds with incredible wingspans and have been propped up with provocative photographs, some of which were obvious hoaxes and others have questioned the very memory of the photo itself.

Then every so often, the legend seems to come alive with another photograph or seemingly outlandish testimony, raising eyebrows, stirring a debate and questioning the possible logical existence of such a creature.

Researcher Cathy Clark has been actively involved behind the scenes of Cryptozoology, outdoor living and animal behavioral for almost five decades. Her interest and personal investigations have lead her to remote locations of Montana and Idaho, the Rocky Mountains of Colorado, forests of Oregon and Washington, the deserts of Arizona, Nevada, New Mexico and Utah to the beautiful shores of California. A natural born naturalist, soaking up volumes of animal behavioral books like a sponge from an early age, Clark then actively pursued field research for her own edification, at times camping in the wilderness for months at a time with little more than a knife and a flashlight on her belt. These camping excursions, she will tell you, "were for the sole purpose to identify a rarely-seen butterfly or glimpse a migrating bird." Her rewards have been realized often with a better personal understanding of how nature works and the excitement she has seen in young people's eyes and heard in their voices as they have asked to see her photographs and hear her stories of nature.

For these reasons, and Cathy Clark's devotion to wildlife, I give you her following personally researched Thunderbird report.

# The Thunderbird Legends by Cathy Clark

The Indian legend of the Thunderbird is thought to be a myth by the civilized modern day population and by many American Indian ancestors we've interviewed. This widely accepted and often-repeated legend believes that Thunderbirds bring storms, their wings flapping causes thunder, and their eyes blinking causes the lightening.

Let us go beyond the myth to examine the possibility of the existence of Thunderbirds. It has been noted by numerous experts that for a bird the alleged size of a Thunderbird to be able to soar, a considerable updraft must be present, which does exist in front of storms. The riding of these updrafts may be what unwittingly had the Indians legend to implicate Thunderbirds as bringing storms with them. Conversely, atmospheric physics show that storms may bring Thunderbirds by providing the necessary environment for such a large bird to soar.

There are those who pass off the sightings by Indians as hallucinations. However, even though Indians used hallucinogens in their ceremonies, they were far from always under the influence and they are as capable of knowing what they saw as anyone else and perhaps more so. As hunter-gatherers, they traveled all over, even into those places we may consider uninhabitable. Therefore, American Indians have historically had far better access to the early wilderness than others have and their sightings and legends should be taken into account when determining the probability of the existence of Thunderbirds.

### American Indian Totem Poles

Thunderbirds, as well as other creatures, are frequently depicted on totem poles. However, I ask if they are random flights of fancy? Totem poles were once carved and raised to represent many things; a family clan, its kinship system, its dignity, its accomplishments, it prestige, its adventures, its stories and its rights and prerogatives. A totem pole served, in essence, as the emblem of a family or clan and often as a reminder of its ancestry. In times past, one main reason a totem was raised was to honor a deceased and respected elder and the rights this person had acquired over their lifetime.

In general, totem poles mean, "This is who we are; these carvings symbolically show what we stand for." Additionally, Natives felt they had special rights to claim a link to the superhuman beings and creatures they depicted on their poles. Some of these special links included, being "descended from ...." or having "recently encountered..." or having "received a gift from..." Some poles embody one-of-a-kind stories or unusual symbols and even to record an encounter with the supernatural. These stories or symbols are known in their entirety only to the pole's owner and the carver of the totem pole. If the pole's owner or carvers gave an account to a relative, granted interviews to academics, or left a written record, these unusual meanings are known, if not, hidden or special meanings have been lost over time.

*Photo courtesy Cathy Clark*

Many poles are topped off with a Thunderbird, sort of a generic capper figure, something like a Christmas star if you will, which often has far less meaning than the carefully thought out symbolic creatures carved into the lower regions. Indians also have other myths that contain fantastic creatures such as cannibal heads, giant heads that roll about eating people, a race of giants they called Flint Coat's with stone for skin who ate people, snake people with snake like features. In addition, the creature called Uktehi by the Lakota and Uktena by the Cherokee was a horned water snake. Others like the Kolowissi (Zuni), a gigantic water snake and the Seminole's Nokos Oma was a "Little Bear", they claimed to be a small bear like animal, Numuzoho by the Ute, Paiute and Shoshone was a one armed, one legged, one-eyed giant that eats people. Maymaygwayshi of the Abenaki Micmac had little people who can walk through, swim through and climb solid stone and the Windigo of Northeast Canadian tribes told of cannibal people. However, these few examples given are mythological creatures and are not usually depicted on totem poles. People, events, real creatures and Thunderbirds often are depicted on Totem Poles.

Thunderbirds depicted on totem poles are not depicted bald like vultures or condors; they are depicted as raptors, which indicate the Indians do not consider them scavengers. However minimal points, these do need to be considered when debating the possibility of the actual existence of Thunderbirds.

### Legends Legacy

It is interesting to note that where reported sightings of Thunderbirds have taken place the local's name buildings, bowling alleys, art galleries and even parks have been named after the creature. This may have at least two implications that requires further examination, first people in these places may be predisposed to believing they see Thunderbirds, which are often mistaken identities of eagles or vultures and secondly, Thunderbirds historically may have existed in these places and may still exist in these places, possibly being seen occasionally.

### Sightings

It is most probable to logically assume with little research needed, that

99% of Thunderbird sightings are misidentifications of condors or vultures by those who have never seen a bird larger than their Thanksgiving turkey. In addition, sightings in populated areas are less likely as more people would see them being in the sky and someone would have clearly photographed the culprit by now. There is more photographic evidence for the existence of UFOs than there is for Thunderbirds.

## Historical Sightings

There are historical accounts of Thunderbird sightings, doubtful we will find any argument here, but these come with no hard evidence at all, except for the testimonies from the eyewitnesses, who are now either, deceased, unavailable for interview or stand fast to their encounter.

**Germany, July 12, 1763:** While in the mountains, a couple left their three-year-old daughter lying asleep by a stream as they cut grass a short distance away. When they went to check on her, they were horrified to find her missing. A frantic search proved fruitless until a man passing by on the other side of the hill heard a child crying. As he went to investigate, he was startled at the sight of a huge eagle flying up before him. At the spot from which it had ascended, he found the little girl, her arm torn and bruised. When the child was reunited with her parents, they and her rescuer estimated that the bird had carried her well over 1,400 feet. The rescuer described the bird as a large eagle, not a vulture. There are no known living eagles that can carry a 3-year-old child in flight.

**French Alps, 1838:** A little girl, five years old, called Marie Delex, was playing with one of her companions on a mossy slope of the mountain, when an eagle swooped down upon her and carried her away in spite of the cries and presence of her young friend. Some adults, hearing the screams, hastened to the spot but sought in vain for the child, they found nothing but one of her shoes on the edge of a precipice. The child had not been carried to the eagle's nest, where only two eaglets were seen surrounded by heaps of goat and sheep bones. It was not until two months later that a shepherd discovered the corpse of Marie Delex, frightfully mutilated, and laying upon a rock half a league from where she had been borne off. Another eagle like bird that flew to considerable height with a 5-year-old child, whose young were found among bones of sheep and goats, which normally weigh in excess of 20 pounds. It is interesting to note that these two events occurred in Europe.

**Tippah County, Mississippi, fall 1868:** A school teacher recorded the following: "A sad casualty occurred at my school a few days ago. The eagles have been very troublesome in the neighborhood for some time past, carrying off pigs, lambs, etc. No one thought that they would attempt to prey upon children; but on Thursday, at recess, the little boys were out some distance from the house, playing marbles, when their sport was interrupted by a large eagle sweeping down and picking up little eight year old Jemmie Kenney." The teacher continued, "When I got out of the house, the eagle was so high that I could just hear the child screaming. The eagle was induced to drop the boy, but its talons had been buried in him so deeply, and the fall was so great, that he was killed."

Some of these sightings are still available in printed form and can be easily found. "**Kentucky, 1870:** A large bird landed on a barn owned by James Pepples in rural Stanford. Pepples fired on the creature, wounding it, and took it into captivity. A contemporary press account says, 'On measurement, the bird proved to be seven feet from tip to tip. It was of a black color, and both similar and dissimilar in many ways, to an eagle.' Nothing is known of its fate."

While a seven-foot wingspan is well within the size of condors and vultures still quite alive on this planet, the rest of this description is very interesting. It is described as being similar and yet dissimilar to an eagle. It is not described as having a long neck or a naked head like a vulture and the people of the time would have been very familiar with vultures, buzzards and eagles as well as the other raptors that were much more numerous in the 1800s than they are today. It is doubtful that this report was a misidentification of a vulture.

Here is another example: "**Alberta, July 1925:** Two visitors to Consolation Valley in the Canadian Rockies spotted what they thought was an eagle at high altitude. As the bird approached the Tower of Babel, a 7500-foot-high peak within the mountain range, they noticed that it was huge and brown, and carried a large animal in its talons. Shouts from the observers caused it to drop the animal, which turned out to be a 15 pound mule-deer fawn."

Many birds could be "huge and brown". However, even the largest known raptor is not capable of flying with a 15-pound fawn in its clutches.

### Modern Sightings

**Puerto Rico, 1975:** During a spate of unexplained nocturnal killings of farm and domestic animals, owners sometimes reported being awakened by a "loud screech" and hearing the flapping of enormous wings. Several witnesses claimed daylight sightings of what one called a "whitish-colored gigantic condor or vulture.

This sighting is specific in the assertion that the bird was a giant form of vulture or condor. However, vultures and condors are scavengers, not raptors (they do not actively hunt large prey), and they usually sleep at night. It is possible for birds and other creatures to develop pituitary problems, which cause gigantism, and it is possible for birds to develop albino and white individuals within a population. The probability of gigantism and whitening occurring simultaneously in the same individual is very slim.

**Northern California, October 1975:** Residents of a Walnut Creek neighborhood saw an immense bird, over five feet tall with a "head like a vulture" and gray wings, dwarfing a nearby eucalyptus tree. Five minutes later, it flew away, revealing a 15-foot wingspan. Around the same time, in nearby East Bay, a number of persons observed the same or a similar bird sitting on a rooftop."

Several people in two different locations made this report. The description of the head and the size could indicate a condor, but in the 1970s, condors in the wild were practically non-existent. This could have been a case of gigantism in an individual vulture.

In 1977 at Lawndale Illinois, a very large bird temporarily abducted Marlon Lowe. A complete account of this incident can be found in *Strange Highways* by Jerry D. Coleman, so reiteration here is unnecessary. However, there is one more aspect of this event to consider. Marlon's mother describes the bird as being all black with a white ring around its neck, a black head and a long beak curved at the end. This description (except for the white ring) matches the reconstruction of Argentavis Magnificens shown at the Los Angeles Museum of Natural History in 1980.

Most people consider the white ring to be indicative of a vulture or condor. However, vultures and condors have unfeathered flesh colored heads. The birds the Lowe's saw had black feathered heads with necks in proportion to the body as eagles are. Vultures and Condors are carrion eaters, scavengers, which are why their heads are bald, and their necks are long in relation to body size, so the carrion is not stuck to the feathers while feeding inside a carcass. As scavengers, they very rarely, if ever, expend energy hunting, and no known vulture is large enough to carry off a 15 pound fawn, much less a 60 pound child.

Raptors (hunting birds) include eagles, hawks, and falcons, falcons are very small, and are colored in varying shades of brown, tan and gray. Hawks are larger, and also colored in varying shades of brown, tan and gray. Eagles are very large and come in a variety of colors, usually shades of brown, tan, gray, and in the case of Bald Eagles (which are not bald) black with white heads. However, none of these raptors is large enough to carry a 60-pound child in flight.

Argentavis Magnificens was also a raptor, and easily large enough to carry off with a 60 pound child. The reconstruction of Argentavis Magnificens looks very much like a giant raven or eagle, and bears no resemblance to a vulture at all. Argentavis Magnificens, and the birds the Lowe's saw, has necks in proportion to the body just as raptors do. Considering these facts, it is very unlikely that a vulture or condor abducted Marlon Lowe.

### Alaskan Sightings

On October 18, 2002, the *Anchorage Daily News* in Alaska reported a sighting of a large bird by pilot John Bouker and a number of his passengers. The article also reported a separate sighting by Moses Coupchiak, a heavy equipment operator. During a personal telephonic interview with John Bouker, he told me, "The large bird looked like a giant golden eagle except the head was different, it had a 'blunt face' plus the beak and head were reminiscent of a King Eider Duck. It had a light colored head and a medium brown body." He also relates that there were seven people in his plane who first saw the bird and pointed it out to him, as well as 20 to 30 witnesses who were on the ground as he landed the plane. Bouker said, "The bird seemed unafraid and circled the plane twice, at one point coming as close as 300 feet to the plane, then circled the people standing on the ground a number of times before flying off." Biologists in the area dismiss the sightings as a Stellars Sea Eagle.

The adult Steller's Sea Eagle is characterized by immense size, dark brown to black plumage with prominent white tail, shoulders, thighs, forehead, and usually crown and a yellow, very deep, strongly arched and compressed beak, the rump, upper and under tail, and under wing coverts white. Eye, cere, and legs are yellow, the tail wedge-shaped. Males and females are similar, but females are noticeably larger. Wing length of females up to 680 mm, males 590. Weight of females up to 9 kg, males 6 kg.

John Bouker was very specific about his description of the large bird, and even though it is possible that it was a Stellars Sea Eagle, three things about his report suggest that it was not a Stellars Sea Eagle. First, his description did not include a white tail or white patches on the wings. Second, Stellars Sea Eagle wingspans are around 8 feet, the bird Bouker and his passengers saw was almost twice that size. Third, the only reason two separate people from two separate sightings would worry about children being outside when this bird is around, would be if it were actually large enough to be capable of carrying off a child.

## Pterodactyls

There are modern accounts of pterodactyl-like creatures dubbed Ropens. We should ask, would it be possible for prehistoric creatures such as Pterodactyls or Argentavis Magnificens to survive into modern times in areas which are uninhabited by man? The fossil record proves the existence of large birds such as Argentavis Magnificens and just like the Coelacanth; they may still exist without our knowledge in the wild places of North and South America.

## Ravens

Ravens are very intelligent birds, related to Magpies and Mynahs. Recently wild Ravens have been documented using automobile traffic to open nuts by dropping them in the path of oncoming traffic, then waiting for the nut to be smashed by a tire. When observed over a period of time, it was discovered that the Ravens figured out that it was safer to drop the nuts into the crosswalk and wait for the light to stop traffic before going into the street to claim their nutmeats. This suggests a greater intelligence than mere instinct. Ravens are not Thunderbirds, but they do bear a striking resemblance to Argentavis Magnificens as reconstructed from the fossil record.

From these observations it could be extrapolated that Argentavis Magnificens may have been of higher than average intelligence for birds. This may help to explain the rarity of sightings of Thunderbirds. Generally, intelligent wild creatures stay away from humans unless they have been around them enough to know that they are safe as with most city dwelling birds. Another example of this is the cougar. Populations of cougars are coming back in the wild, but sightings of cougars are still relatively rare and cause for excitement when sighted. It is well within the realm of possibility that a breeding population of Thunderbirds could exist and remain hidden from humans by intelligent choice, caution, or instinct.

### Known Species

It should be noted that the reports of giant birds vary from looking like vultures to looking like eagles, and some even claimed to resemble pterodactyls. Due to these different creatures all being lumped in together as a Thunderbird sighting, the search for these winged majesties has been confused. Therefore, it is required that a separate description be made for Thunderbird.

The possibilities for Thunderbird species are Albatross, gigantic Vultures or Condors (scavengers), gigantic Eagles (raptors), large Pterodactyls (raptors), or species like Argentavis Magnificens (raptors).

It is possible that Albatross have been mistaken for Thunderbirds in sightings that happened along the coast, but it is doubtful that Albatross would be present during inland sightings as they are strictly sea-going birds. A scavenger is unlikely to be the Thunderbird due to the predation aspect of Thunderbirds, which leaves three raptors.

A Pterodactyl is unlikely to be the Thunderbird, as they do not bear feathers, although it is possible that Pterodactyls will still exist in the most remote places on the planet, only basing this assumption on the number of sightings of Pterodactyl-like creatures reported in the past 200 years.

Gigantic eagles may be the Thunderbird, the sightings and abduction accounts certainly resemble a giant eagle's active predation.

Argentavis Magnificens is a very likely candidate for the Thunderbird. Its size and shape (specifically length of neck in proportion to the body) resemble many reports of Thunderbirds. So when discussing Thunderbirds as a species, we must agree that we are not discussing Vultures or Condors or Pterodactyls, we are in fact discussing a gigantic raptor resembling an Eagle. All other species must be considered separate species or gigantic individuals of known species, and not to be confused with Thunderbirds. The European sightings do appear to be Thunderbirds according to this criterion, and it is very possible for a subspecies or separate species of gigantic eagle like raptor to exist outside of the Americas.

### Food Sources

It is known that large animals can live on small meals, whales live on krill, and wolves live on mice. It is possible for a Thunderbird to exist on the mammals within its territory, from small ones like marmots to large ones like deer. It is probable that Thunderbirds prefer larger prey, boars etc. However, when such large food sources are unavailable, it is very possible that Thunderbirds resort to smaller fare, rabbits etc. Breeding due to their size, Thunderbirds would be long lived, breed slowly and only need 500 to 1000 individuals to maintain a viable breeding population, particularly in vast uninhabited mountainous terrain, which could sustain multiple territories.

### Habitat

It is possible for a large bird to remain among peaks and canyons of uninhabited mountains without human knowledge except for very few actual sightings of which are generally passed over as hallucination or misidentification. With this in mind, it is very logical that no physical evidence has been found so far.

### Migration Paths

The main question asked is why no bird watchers have seen a Thunderbird. This is a very good question. Recent sightings have occurred in Alaska, Texas, and Illinois. It is understood that in order for a bird of such size to soar there must be sufficient air movement. For these birds to migrate there must exist sufficient air movement across a vast span of atmosphere that encompasses Alaska, Texas, and Illinois. There is one event that accomplishes this, the Jet Stream. It is possible that Thunderbirds migrate on the jet stream, causing them to be unnoticed by most people, too far up to be seen. The only problem with this idea is that airlines frequently use the jet stream, and none has reported seeing a Thunderbird, nor has any anomalous radar pick up been reported in the jet stream. Radar has picked up clouds of smaller birds, insects and bats in the jet stream and it is possible that an anomalous Thunderbird blip could have been passed off as a cloud of any of these flocks mentioned.

### Paranormal

It is sometimes suggested that those who report seeing Thunderbirds either were under the influence and saw a hallucination, or saw a ghost or angel. It is very possible that some sightings will be due to hallucination produced by intoxicants. However, the Alaskan pilot was not intoxicated while flying his plane when he and his passengers viewed the giant bird in the sky. It may be possible for some sightings to be ghosts or angels, but these apparitions rarely stay around for very long and are usually seen by only one or two people in a group. In addition, apparitions such as ghosts and angels, being incorporeal, do not carry off children or full-grown beasts and people. It is unlikely that Thunderbirds are anything more than a natural animal.

### Possibility

Human population densities make the probability of a breeding population of Thunderbirds within the lower 48 states very unlikely. They would have been documented by ornithologists, photographed by numerous people, and seen by many people much as people see a Piper Cub airplane over a vast area while it is flying high in the sky. However, much of Alaska is unpopulated due to most of it being inaccessible by anything less than an airplane or helicopter. It is very possible, even likely, that a breeding population of Thunderbirds exist in the wilds of Alaska, undiscovered due to the inhospitable terrain, occasionally seen while hunting, rarely, if ever, reported by Inuit's who probably consider it to be a normal animal just like Polar Bears and would see no reason to report it to anyone. If Argentavis Magnificens or a relative has managed to survive to the present day, Alaska is most likely where they will be found.

-------------------------------------------------------------------------------------------

   Cathy Clark's contribution of her personal research, interviews, time and theories for this chapter on Thunderbirds is indeed a very constructive tool to use in one's own research and investigations. Studying and comparing notes from other researchers, and considering other theories, can never be deemed as a wasted enterprise. Although, I do not agree with some of her conclusions or consider the actual existence of a living, breeding Argentavis Magnificens, it is as they say, "No matter how thin the pancake, theres always two sides!"

   My investigations related to thunderbird, or big bird sightings, have taken a hands-on approach, keeping the speculation at bay. Over the course of the last four decades, I've personally interviewed scores of alleged Thunderbird witnesses and have yet to find any conclusive proof, or as far as that goes, any circumstantial evidence, that could point to an undiscovered, unknown, extremely large bird. Hundreds of man hours have been allocated to area searches for nests, roosting locations, photographic documentation,possible prey inspection and any physical evidence left behind such as feathers or scat. Nothing, aside from some valid testimony, has been found.

   Would I agree that these Thunderbird witnesses are seeing a large bird? Absolutely... first, the witnesses never refers to their sighting as "Thunderbird" only as "an unknown large bird" or something very similar. Second, the witness seldom seeks out the media or researchers and more times than not, these stories come from local word of mouth. Most convincing are the thousands of bird-watching amateurs and experts that never report a thunderbird sighting.

   In many cases, Thunderbird research begins and ends with the inconsistency of the stories and what these flying culprits may be. Could the Red-crowned Crane, which stands almost 5 feet tall or the Wondering Albatross, that has a wing span exceeding 11 and 1/2 feet, or the California Condor, which is North America's largest flying bird, with a body length of 53 inches and wing span of  9 and 1/2 feet, quite possible be the modern day Thunderbird?

   It's hard to say but many researchers tend to dismiss these birds as too unlikely. Too unlikely? Such dismissal only begs another question --- can we consider an unknown or extinct species or prehistoric bird to be more likely?

# 6. STRANGE BUT REAL

Throughout the years, four decades to be precise I have placed myself on trails, in forests and prairies, wading through streams, canoeing down rivers, climbing mountains, camping in snow blizzards, sitting in tree stands and hiking to remote locations and forgotten places simply to observe nature's unique creatures. Fortunately, animal oddities have been stumbled across many times.

In the 1960's, scores of six-legged frogs were found at Faries Park on the far east side of Decatur, Illinois. In fact, during that summer it seemed more difficult to find a normal four-legged frog at that little pond than it was to capture a six-legged leaper. Of course, scientists have since determined that a parasite causes this deformity in frogs but at the time it was quite a discovery for a young lad.

Another time, I captured a four and one-half foot long green iguana as it basked in the sun at a secluded location overlooking an Illinois river. Years after the iguana was captured, I saw what looked like a dead shark float past my campsite at Sangchris (freshwater) Lake in central Illinois. Grabbing the net and jumping into a little raft, I rowed after the fish and discovered it to be in fact a 3 foot-long nurse shark.

This section is included here for two important reasons. First, and most obvious, not every known animal we see or experience is always understood. Some creatures, seen at a glance, heard from afar or even witnessed for long minutes may be, have been and will be at times, misidentified creatures, escaped/released pets, hybrids or mutants.

Be aware that a total and complete understanding as either witness or researcher needs to exist. You can only testify to fact, not leaping to a creature of the edge because an animal walked on two legs or a strange little furious thing screamed as it leaped from a tree --- just because we assume that cats do not act like that and dogs cannot walk like that. Well, yes they can act like that and have acted like that on numerous occasions. Many other known animals behave and appear at different times and under unusual circumstances. The question here is not "what" --- but "why".

The second reason demands the reporting of these unique or confused y-creatures so we can be totally aware of not only the possibility of their behavior and appearance but the fact that these known creatures may be the logical and correct explanation to the thought-to-be unknown encounter.

These animals, classified as Y-creatures (why are they there and/or why do some act as they do?), have subcategories like LOCO"S ( Locals Out of Control and Often Sighted) and LOSTT (Locals OutSide Their Territory,) and their appearance goes deeper and means more than the simple quick "Out Of Place" (OOP) meaningless term so many wish to utilize. Not only is the OOP umbrella too simple a term but extremely incorrect. To conclude an animal OOP, and the case is closed, is wrong. One must transform the OOP to the more correct term, Y-creature, where a unique, individual examination of the event must be investigated.

Too often these glimpses, shadows and sounds of animals we see and hear are immediately cataloged as cryptids (unknown, undiscovered animals). This quick jump to judgment is not only extremely unscientific but very counterproductive in the legitimate quest for answers in Cryptozoology. One should consider every animal of the area, and then consider every known beast of the world, before leaping to an undiscovered, unknown critter.

To demonstrate the wide variety of known mammals and larger birds, I know to exist within a five mile radius of this rather secluded, yet civilized East Tennessee countryside I call home, I've assembled quite a lengthy list.

On the 'domesticated' side, there are cats, dogs, cows, horses, donkeys, llamas, bison, hogs, chicken, sheep, goats, peacocks, African guineas, ferrets, and even a young chimpanzee. Then on the 'wild' side, around these parts, you'll find feral cats and dogs, mink, beaver, otter, muskrat, groundhogs, opossum, raccoons, squirrels, rabbits, chipmunks, fox, coyote, bobcat, deer, wolves, bear, black vultures, turkey vultures, wild turkeys, herons, Canadian geese, owls, eagles, hawks, bats and the list goes on and on.

One must also consider the animals kept by exotic handlers (as the chimpanzee mentioned above). According to Rick Foret owner of G & R Aviary of Raceland, Louisiana, "The United States presently has 4700 legally registered exotic keepers, however, over 15,000 animals a year illegally enter the country and that translates into a multi-million dollar smuggling industry." With that said, you may be surprised how long the list of animals is for the area you reside in. So, consider all the 'knowns' before assuming an unknown.

## Creek Critter

One of my earliest experiences of a Y-creature occurred some time in the early 1960's, while fishing on the outskirts of Decatur, Illinois in Stevens Creek. My friend, Kenny and I had fought our way well off the beaten path to an isolated bend in the creek, a place where the waterway took a 90-degree turn, thus creating a large calm pond-like area. There was no path to this hidden location, evidenced by the lack of human debris like beer cans, pop bottles around it, and we truly enjoyed this pristine place. Even though it had taken a good hour to get to the peaceful creeks eddy, fighting the brush, swatting the bugs and crossing the creek from side to side when the bank became nothing more than a steep embankment, we thought this pocket of privacy would provide us with fish we longed to catch. We were soon to get our wish -- but in a way that we did not expect.

Baiting the hook and casting to the center of the pond-like area, my line immediately went tight, dragging the rod and reel into the water and it vanished without warning! Amazed and surprised, Kenny quickly readied his tackle and cast. Within seconds, his line went tight and snapped his pole in two. My pole was now seen drifting up the creek and around the bend. I hurriedly went to retrieve it and inspected the damage. Something had taken the bait, 'hook, line and sinker' but the rod and tackle was no worse for the wear.

We soon realized that we had better make some adjustments to our gear since it was obvious that the fish doing the damage was not the usual blue gill, catfish and perch that we were accustomed to catching upstream. So, we set our drags wide open, upgraded our line to a heavier test, put on larger hooks and cast the bait back into the water. Almost the same thing happened again. The fish took the bait, darted from one end of the pond to the other, then came towards to bank and stopped, leaving plenty of slack in the line. When we started to reel it in, a snag would be felt and then --- pop --- the line would snap. The fish was apparently swimming under some emerged debris, wrapping the line tight, then snapping free. This happened over and over again, mo matter what we tried. Admittedly, big time anglers we were not.

Soon, we were out of heavy tackle and went to tell our incredible fish story to Kenny's big brother, Tommy. Tommy listened quietly as he rubbed his chin then went to the garage, as he yelled, "You punks better not be lying!" He threw his fishing gear in his trunk along with a row of clothesline and a dog chain then we rushed back to the creek. On the way to the creek, Tommy was trying to believe us, but honestly, I could tell he did not. His questions were understandably skeptical but he finally concluded that if what we were saying was true than we had to have found one huge damn fish!

When we arrived at the creek, Tommy got his rod and reel ready as Kenny and I stood back and watched. Within a minute, the same thing happened to Tommy. He swore and Kenny and I smirked as we exclaimed in unison that we had told him so. Irritated, Tommy took out his heavy stuff and demanded Kenny and I go and get a long branch and find out how deep the water was. Our first stick was just over six feet long did not touch bottom. Our next branch measured over ten feet long and still did not touch bottom. Then, getting a stick and measuring it by again by marking Tommy's height to the stick, it was well over 14 feet in length, we seemed to hit the soft creek bottom this time.

Tommy was now on a mission, determined to catch the stubborn fish, or whatever the critter was, and it appeared we were ill-matched. The evening was setting in and it would be a long hike back in the pitch dark if we did not leave soon, so plans were made to return the next morning.

Tommy and Kenny picked me up the next day now poised, hyped and prepared to land our local creek monster. After numerous attempts, Tommy got the fish on the shore, it was huge! At the time, I had never seen such a fish and certainly would have never dreamed that such a fish would be in this little creek. After catching the monster, and chaining it to the bank, Tommy cast out repeatedly -- and the same problems with broken lines continued to occur. This meant that there was another fish, maybe even larger, still out there in the water. We decided to be satified with the one we had caught though and packed up and departed. Who knows what we left behind?

We later confirmed that the fish we had caught was a 55 pound German Carp that was 42 inches long. Why was it there? How did it get there? I have always felt another angler must have placed it there. But a feeling is only assumption.

**Update:** A trip back to that little hidden spot Kenny and I discovered in 1962 was taken September 15, 2003. Much to my amazement the location was still untouched. The bend and the deep pocket of water in Steven's Creek was as I had left it 40 years earlier. I was sitting there quietly on the bank and couldn't help but notice the large swirls that were moving about in the water. Had the huge carp made it into the next millennium?

## The Sangamon River Monster

Back in 1980, if you had visited the banks of the Sangamon River by Oakley, Illinois, you would have found an old man living on a nearby farm the local kids called, "Mister Moe" Mr. Moe would constantly warn the children not to ever venture into the woods behind the house. He could often be found standing by his fence telling tales of finding two of his dogs in the woods with their heads torn off or of piles of meat that he had placed outside quickly disappearing overnight.

Moe told the kids a large monster lived on his property, back in the woods, he claimed, not far from the river and would constantly warn the young ones to never, ever go back to the woods! He had seen it more than once, he would tell them. The thing was about 7 feet tall, could hide in the trees, was all covered with hair and loved to eat meat. Other than these scary warnings, Moe was friendly with the kids and often invited them over for campfire cookouts but would always remind them to never enter the woods --- not ever.

By complete chance, I heard about these dire warnings while fueling at a nearby gas station. One child that I interviewed told me Mr. Moe had once shown him a shredded rabbit that he had claimed was the work of the creature. Immediately, I went to Mister Moe's home to request an interview.

Moe answered the door and was quite pleasant and even asked me inside, followed by an offer of a soda. After my introduction, and a bit of small talk, I asked Moe about the creature he talked about that lived in his woods. Moe told me he believed it to be a bobcat in reality, but made up the story of a huge monster to assure himself the children would not explore the area.

Almost sounding logical on the surface, I could sense he was holding back something. Before I could ask the next question, Moe said, "I'd take you back there but the poison ivy is horrible at this time of year, its just awful, I don't want to be sued or anything."

I assured him that I would never sue him and would steer clear of the poison ivy.

"Well, to be honest," he then said, "I just rent this land and the landlord said to keep everyone off the property. So, as much as I'd like to take you back there and search for the cat, I just can't."

Then strangely, I thought, he refused to tell me who owned the property. Graciously, I thanked him for his time and left the premises --- and went directly to a neighbor's house about two miles up the road. I obtained the name and telephone number of the landowner of Moe's house, who was now identified as a man named Drakes. When I contacted him, he told me that Moe rented only the house and one acre of land. The woods that stretched back to the river were not leased to Moe. Quickly, I asked for permission to investigate the area behind the house. Drakes stated he could not grant the request because it would entail trespassing through Moe's leased land in order to gain access to the woods. I then suggested entering the woods via the river by boat. Drakes agreed to this with one stipulation, that he accompany me. Drakes stated: "If there is a bobcat or bobcat family back in there I want to get rid of it, I have livestock in the area!"

One week later, I met the property owner, Drakes at the Faries Park boat ramp on Lake Decatur, approximately 10 miles by water from our destination. As we closed in from the river, I killed the boat motor about a quarter mile from the woods and Moe's house then paddled the rest of the way so as not to scare anything or alert Moe of our approach.

When we reached the shore of the wooded area, we docked the boat and started a long hike into the heavily overgrown woods. Little conversation was taking place until Drakes pulled out a .38 caliber revolver he had been carrying in his small cooler. He smiled and said, "this is just for our protection, if the cats are back here I just want them caught and released somewhere else."

I sighed and said, "chances are we won't see a thing, except perhaps some tracks."

About 15 to 20 minutes passed as we were weaving our way through the woods and then, as if a curtain had opened in the forest, we walked into a a large brightly lit clearing. This well hidden, cultivated space was full of 7-foot tall marijuana plants! It seemed that we had found Mister Moe's "seven foot monsters"!

Drakes asked me to take a few photographs then promptly confronted Moe with what had been found. For me, it was filed as another "excuse" used to create a creature. A conjured-up monster that most of the local children, and perhaps even some adults, will always believe existed as the Sangamon River Monster.

Note: Names were changed in this account for legal reasons.

## Y- Creature Bird: Case Closed

It was a beautiful summer day in 1988. I was putting my son down for a nap in his upstairs bedroom when my eyes caught something colorful outside his window. Creeping over to the window, I spotted a parakeet on the roof. I assumed that someone's pet got loose, but soon another one landed next to the first. I looked around and two more of the same breed of parakeets were seen in a nearby tree.

What in the world? Why would there be loose parakeets so far north as Elgin, Illinois? I tried to reason it out. Are the birds wild, migrating and lost or did a truck that was transporting them have an accident and lose its cargo? Then, I recalled another time years ago, in 1971, when I had seen this same type of parakeet flying wild and free in Southern Illinois. The 1971 sighting I quickly had logged, filed and forgot about, again assuming it was nothing more than another pet escapee.

This is your classic Y-creature, sub classification LOSTT, sighting with true and documented facts to close the case. It was the Monk Parakeet, native to South America, now with known feral colonies existing and thriving in the United States. Monk Parakeets have been nesting as far north as Hyde Park a suburb of Chicago since the late 60's or early 70's.

Feral colonies were first reported in the late 1960's from Texas and Florida to New York and Illinois. Expert Michelle Lawson stated, "In a major avian fiasco, crates containing Monk Parakeets were broken open at Kennedy airport and contributed to the initial spread."

## The Piebald Deer

Outside of hunting circles this rarely talked about animal is seldom spoke of or even known to the general public. A genetic mutation, termed piebald, or as many pronounce it in the south "pie-ball", is an animal with patches of usually brown and white, as is seen in painted horses.

*White-tailed Piebald Deer, Courtesy Earl Leblanc*

Word of a large piebald buck, which was being spotted locally, reached me during the summer of 2003. Witnesses stated that an almost solid white, ten-point buck was being seen often in an unincorporated industrial park of

Surgoinsville, Tennessee. Immediately, I scheduled a trip to the area in hopes of confirming the existence of the deer.

On September 22, I was able to interview Mr. Herman Johnson, the superintendent in charge of the industrial park. I explained to Mr. Johnson that I hoped to confirm the existence of the piebald deer, detailing the numerous hours and distance that I had already put into the quest.

Johnson, or as he calls himself, "The Guardian of the Pie-ball", told me many stories of the deer and it was obvious that he had become enchanted with it. Years ago, when Johnson had first seen the piebald, there were two of them, twins, he said. One of them was killed a year later, the victim of a nearby highway, and while it did not have as much white on it as the remaining animal, the coloring was still noticeable, Johnson told me.

He had spent countless hours fending off hunters, who trespassed in the area on midnight runs and on one occasion even tricked Johnson into believing they were from the forestry department. Johnson jerked a cell phone out of his right front pocket like a gunslinger drawing a .45 and said, "I don't mess around with them anymore. I call the Sheriff!"

Johnson spoke of the piebald like a proud father would speak of his children. "I recall just last spring watching the pie-ball going from one doe to the next and boy, were they waiting in line for him!"

I asked him if he had seen any of the piebald's young and he replied, "I'd venture a guess that most all the young deer in this park are his, but if you're asking have any of the fawns been white and brown, I did find one that must have died at birth with a few large patches of white on it."

Johnson then took me to a restricted area deep in the interior of the park. He pulled his vehicle over, slowly opened his door as he quietly leaned over to me and said, "This is where I feed my deer everyday." Then he bounced up like on a spring and yelled, "Here, little deer! Here, little deer!"

After the shock of his unexpected scream wore off, I was amazed to see a number of deer coming out of the forest's edge and cautiously strolling toward the vehicle.

Looking deeper into the woods, I could see many more fawns and a few young bucks hanging back, but no piebald. Johnson then leaped into the back of his pick-up truck and started tossing out pumpkins. I joined the task and soon we were both sitting on the tail-gate slicing a bucket of apples in two and throwing the fruit at the deer.

Johnson asked if I wanted to help him get the next load of pumpkins and feed them next week. Of course, I agreed, and met him back at his industrial park office the following Saturday. As we drove back to the secluded feeding area, Johnson told me he had already taken an earlier load, hoping to pull in more deer for me to see. It had worked, for when the vehicle cleared the ridge and the open meadow was exposed, there stood over 30 deer forgaing in the fruit that he had placed earlier. Again, my eyes located a few shy animals in the forest.

But then there it was, slowly and deliberately emerging from the shadows, the huge almost magical-looking piebald buck! He boldly walked past the vehicle and stood atop a raised incline overlooking his kingdom. I truly was in awe at the sight of this unique animal.

# The Coydog

The term "coydog" is used to describe a wild coyote and domestic dog hybrid. Coydogs were once believed to be found in great numbers throughout southern Illinois, southern Indiana, Ohio and into Pennsylvania. This belief was due to the once expanding coyote population having difficulty finding same species mates. More likely, most of these reported coydogs were true coyotes or feral dogs, since the breeding cycles of dogs and coyotes are not synchronized. Scientific studies have confirmed coyote-dog interbreeding rarely occurs. If it was happening regularly we should be seeing coyotes with domestic dog-like characteristics such as spots, curly tails and floppy ears, which is just not the case. In addition, it is highly likely that red, black and blond coyotes were mistakenly identified as coydogs in the past simply because their coats were not of the more common tri-color pelage.

However, coydogs do exist and should be considered when attempting to identify a seldom seen, off colored, elusive canine-like animal. In my book *Strange Highways*, one will find the first documented report of a coydog in northern Illinois and since that conformation, two other coydogs have been sighted and confirmed.

## Tennessee's Chupacabra

On the afternoon of August 26, 2004, a friend stopped by to shoot the breeze and as always talked about the latest news of our valley neighbors. After talking awhile about the weather and current affairs he said, "Hey ,did you hear about Ike's goat?" I had not and asked him to elaborate.

"You know he's got two goats up there... well, he used to have two goats. Yesterday Ike went out behind his house and found one of them with it's throat torn out and its stomach ripped open, dead as a door nail! Ike didn't know what would kill the goat in that manner but figured whatever it was, came out of the mountains behind his place," he told me.

The Chupacabra, also called the "Goat Sucker", is alleged to kill small animals, many of which are goats, then drain its victim's blood. The creature's name originated in Puerto Rico after the discovery of a number of goats that had been killed. The Chupacabra continues to be reported in Mexico and Puerto Rico today. At the height of the Goat Sucker scare, *UFO Magazine* (March/April 1996) reported that there were more than 2,000 cases of animal mutilations in Puerto Rico in 1994 and 1995 attributed to the Chupacabra.

Witness descriptions of the Chupacabra vary widely. The more popular identifications report a half dinosaur / half alien vampire with quills running down its back. Others claim to have seen a panther-like animal with a long snake-like tongue and scaly skin, while others allege the animal hops, flies and can run at astounding speeds, leaving a sulfuric stench in its wake.

The Chupacabra has a suspicious background of bizarre witness testimony, wild theory and sketchy evidence. Some believe the Goat Sucker to be a United States government experiment gone bad, others lean toward the alien creature theory and still others honestly endorse the Chupacabra as a real, living, undiscovered animal.

This much I am sure of ---- if Ike's goat had been killed in Mexico or Puerto Rico the goat slaying would have been credited to the Chupacabra. But this wasn't Puerto Rico, this was Tennessee, and I never take anything for granted so I went directly over to Ike's house to interview him and investigate the scene.

Needless to say, I never mentioned the Chupacabra. We both discussed the wolves that had been coming down off the mountain. I told Ike that earlier in the summer I had seen a lone wolf frequenting the area. It would stroll quietly down a fence line and stealthily search for food at the large dumpster found at the end of the road. The third time I spotted the wolf, I noticed a rear leg injury, thus adding to my speculation that the wolf is not overly bold. He was simply looking for an easy meal.

Not long after my investigation of Ike's goat, Farris Sensabaugh told me about another neighbor, Ralph Bailey, who had recently lost a small calf. It was beginning to seem that a "flap" might be developing but an interview with Ralph quickly squashed that notion. Mr. Bailey stated his calf had died from black leg disease. Ralph was informed about the evening wolf visits and stated, "Well, this time it was black leg, but next time it may be the wolves. I also have two young goats so I'll be on the look-out for them. maybe I'll set a trap."

The red wolf (Canis rufus) is 1 of 3 species of wild Canis found in North America. The captive-breeding program was extremely successful and the first mainland repatriation of red wolves began in 1987 at the Alligator River National Wildlife Refuge. Subsequent to that, wolves have been released on Bulls Island in South Carolina (1987), Horn Island in Mississippi (1989), St. Vincent Island in Florida (1990), and Great Smoky Mountains National Park in Tennessee (1991). The Great Smoke Mountain National Park Red Wolf Project was cancelled in October 1998 due to hybridization problems with coyotes.

In late July 2004, I started closely monitoring the wolf's appearance, which became as scheduled as the sounds of the evening insects. Every night between 10:30 and 11:00 p.m., the injured wolf would make its way down the fence line, cut across a small field, disappear behind a barn and emerge on a narrow road headed to the dumpster.

On August 1, my son, Nick and I awaited the evening sighting of the lame wolf but something different occurred that night. The time was 10:45 p.m. and just like clock-work, the wolf appeared and quietly, yet alertly weaved its way down the familiar path. I nudged Nick and said, "There it is, see it there by the tree line?"

"Yes, I see it, Nicjk replied, "but what's that on the hill?"

On the hill stood another wolf, this one mostly black in color with patches of gray and white on it. Since that first sighting, we have now seen the black wolf many times, always watching over the lame wolf's journey. I would surmise the dark-colored wolf has always been there, overseeing its mate's quest for food. I would further surmise that these wolves, possible hybrids, killed Ike's goat.

# 7. CRYPTOZOOLOGY 101

**C**ryptozoology yields a potpourri of theories. We find ourselves asking questions when we are fully aware that there are no answers or asking questions that might raise an internal or external debate. Still other Cryptozoological answers are so obvious that the questions never have been seriously asked aloud, thus leaving the answers ambiguous at best.

First, let us go back to the basic question and understand what is Cryptozoology in the first place? Simply put, Cryptozoology comes from the Greek "kruptos", meaning "hidden", and "zoology" being a branch of biology that studies animals. Thus, Crypto-zoology means "the study of hidden animals".

In order for Cryptozoology to ever be considered a true science, it is up to the present day Cryptozoologists to make the efforts that will become recognized to this end. A few Cryptozoologists will simply argue that Cryptozoology is much more than a specialized hobby and should already be taken seriously by the scientific community. They suggest Cryptozoology should now be considered a legitimate and respected science, claiming that scientific methods are used to arrive at their deductions and collect their evidence. Furthermore, they will point out the fact that a few actual doctors and scholars have, at one time or another, acknowledged Cryptozoology. But come on, doctors, scholars, film makers, zoologists and naturalists believe in, and at times take an interest in, stamp collecting and flying model airplanes as well. Interest is not a confirmation that a hobby is a science. A statement by a zoologist that Bigfoot "may exist" does not automatically endorse a Cryptozoologist's status or for that matter, the cryptid itself. And being a consultant on a movie does not equate to a director's or producer's 'belief' in the featured cryptid.

But grabbing at these straws is too often what some Cryptozoologist's do --- fooling themselves. What Cryptozoology needs is less ranting about what it should be and more effort to make it what it could be.

I find it unecessary, and equally irrelevant, to place the title "Cryptozoologist" in the same sentence as my name even though I have to admit that my field research, documentation and investigations, all conducted since the mid 1970's, has earned me a title I do not seek. However, in early 2004, the popular web site Cryptozoology.com created a poll entitled, "Which Cryptozoologist contributed the most in the decade 1990 to 2000?" and I was surprised to be included on a list that contained a number of individuals who I have respected throughout the years. The list included such luminaries as the late Dr. Grover Krantz, professor of Anthropology at Washington State University and the respected newspaper man of British Columbia, John Green. I was further suprised and honored to receive enough votes to place me directly behind the famous Belgian zoologist and highly respected "Father of Cryptozoology", the late Bernard Heuvelmans! I was thrilled to have been listed in third place, not because of the votes received but because of the prestigious company I was in."

## Cryptozoology Q & A

The most frequently asked questions that I receive about becoming a Cryptozoologist are the following:

### 1. How do I become a Cryptozoologist?

At this time, there are no academic programs for, and no academic departments in, Cryptozoology at any credited university or college in existence, save for a few basic courses found in obscure locations. Since no college yet can hand you a degree in Cryptozoology, some individuals may think less of one who uses the term "Cryptozoologist" rather than another "ist". But what college did the person that discovered fire go to? How many degrees did the person that constructed the first wheel hold? And please tell me, what college did the those who the first pyramid graduate from? So in short who needs the "ist" and what does it really matter?

Your interests lie in finding, studying and investigating animals unrecognized by modern science and your search for this too often starts with the search for the title or position of Cryptozoologist. Why worry about titles? Spend your time doing the field work instead.

However, if this is what you seek, the first method to obtain the self-proclaimed status of a Cryptozoologist is to become actively devoted to Cryptozoology and have a thorough understanding of the field. To be taken seriously .one must decide where their interests will be displayed and grow. Studying related course's such as Zoology and Anthropology are a great start.

It is a quick and simple claim to think of yourself, and call yourself, a Cryptozoologist, but only when others refer to you as such, havign earned the designation, is such a title actually worth having.

### 2. What exactly does a Cryptozoologist do?

Many Cryptozoologists write books and articles about the topic, make radio and television guest appearances on the subject and at times even produce their own documentaries on cryptids, always trying to get the word out and inform the public on the secret world of cryptids.

Other Cryptozoologist's maintain a behind-the-scenes mode, investigating and researching independently for years, gathering material and evidence, not only in the field but also in libraries and from newspaper archives. They may also frequent conferences and join or create Cryptozoology interest groups on the web or within their community.

However, the main purpose for a Cryptozoologist is to stay focused, unbiased and personally seek out the truth. A Cryptozoologist is never a follower. He or she is a team player or independent investigator, disciplining one's self to allow the facts of a case to speak for themselves. Then ,if desired, presenting a theory in a clear and concise method.

### 3. Can I earn a living as a Cryptozoologist?

This is a personal question that only you can answer. If you are wondering if there is an application somewhere to fill out and send off for a Crytozoology job ---- the answer at this time is no. Although, you may wish to pursue a career as an investigative reporter for Cryptozoological or Paranormal-type magazines such as *Fate* or *Fortean Times*, most Cryptozoologists become self-proprietors. They create a small business-like operation through book sales, guest appearances and by becoming production advisors.

The hard truth to the fact is you will, in all reality, need a full time occupation to not only earn a living but also to subsidize your Cryptozoology quest. Try your best to make that needed job as complimentary to your interest in Cryptozoology as possible. This may be as simple as acquiring employment that requires/allows travel. Other jobs that entail interaction with the public, computers or allows you plenty of time off, can all be a plus.

Here are some of the jobs I have had over the years, which I feel not only allowed my Cryptozoology interests to stay intact but contributed to my Cryptozoology growth. I became a paramedic, which not only granted me ample time off but put me in direct contact with "excited" eyewitnesses that I could study and interview. Next, I took a job as a production manager for a printing press and here I was able to learn the behind the scenes methods of publications. Another career choice I made with Cryptozoology in mind was becoming an over-the-road owner-operator of a semi-truck, thus giving me the freedom to travel where and when I wanted, going to the latest cryptid sighting, investigating, interviewing and documenting cases in person. Then, again with Cryptozoology in mind, I went after and acquired employment as a counselor for troubled teenagers. This gave me further experience into witness testimony, granted me added experience on camping excursions and wildlife outings and gave me much needed time off to devote to Cryptozoology.

The latest addition to my resume was working as a private investigator for a law film. This career choice was solely based on my interest in Cryptozoology and constructively mixed searching, interviewing and data collection and documentation with the freedom to travel between cases, or even at times, because of cases. Although I have yet to cage Bigfoot or cast a net over Nessie at Loch Ness, I can proudly claim success with notification of copyright infringements, the safe return of two teenagers to their families and the documented whereabouts of three men who owed large amounts of child support. You will find your own path to take that best suits your personal situation.

For me though, actual income received from Cryptozoological- related ventures have been nominal at best. In fact, an accountant would tally the expenses to profit as just about breaking even. Other than a number of articles that I have freelanced throughout the years, the *Myth or Real* collector card set that was created and produced in 1994, the book sales, television production assistance and the personal appearances that I have been paid for, it's all been for the science, not the bank account.

I've also taken serious steps to reach out to other groups seeking or sharing answers and have found knowledge and adventure as the reward. The groups I proudly chose to donate my time to, and share Cryptozoological and Fortean investigations with, are Boy and Girl Scout troops, church and community social gatherings and high school science classes.

Cryptozoology to me is about information, confirmation, documentation and investigation not the monetary returns. If plentiful monetary gains is your driving force you're definitely entering the wrong field.

## *Cryptozoologists in General*

Some Cryptozoologist act as though they have all the answers to the unknown, unanswerable topics of the field. These once few, but now growing numbers of researchers, seem to know almost everything (just ask them!) and can fill in the gaps of what they don't know with weird, unique, unscientific theories. Consider for a moment a doctor of medicine who has all the answers without an examination, would you trust them? Would you go to a Doctor of Dental Surgery to look at a sore back? So, why should a Cryptozoologist know everything equally and completely about everything from Mngwa to Woadd-El-Uma and Ogopogo to Morgawr? Some Cryptozoologists will not draw this professional line and admit what's not within their field of expertise. In fact, they will talk as an expert on any given topic from Chupacabras to the Tasmanian Wolf to Ghosts, UFO's and even have the arrogance to predict the future of Cryptozoology-related events!

Many of these types of Cryptozoologists know that the more they theorize, and the more outlandish those theories are, the more attention they will get. They believe that the attention, no matter where it comes from, makes them appear to be more credible. The more they spew forth, the more they lead Cryptozoology into the land of fiction.

For instance, if I heard a Cryptozoologist say, "Sorry, I'm not familiar with all the facts of that particular cryptid. Most of my research and personal investigation has been geared toward winged creatures." How refreshing would that be? The elements of the human ego and motive are too often overlooked in this field, debates rage on and theories based on opinions are pulled out of the air. Some of these self-appointed experts have even been known to create a completely new species, or sub-species, based on a single anonymous and undocumented encounter! They are becoming storytellers, rather than scientific researchers.

It's up to the rest of us to get Cryptozoology back to the factual basics!

## Conspiracy & Debate

Whether we like it, choose to ignore or just simply care not to believe it, conspiracies are linked to Cryptozoology and the paranormal on a regular basis. These unexplained topics of interest unwillingly invite the "predators of attention". What may be a unique but simple publicized sighting of a large unknown bird is guaranteed to be on someone's plate to give an added dramatic twist of the event or a false-witnessed copycat sighting, given time. Conspiracies take as many forms as the creatures and events encountered, from the thought-to-be harmless white lies told by eyewitnesses to the downright appalling total fabrications enveloping an entire event. Profit is thought to be the overwhelming motive for the conspirators but pause for a moment and consider "the game".

It is the game, which drives these individuals forward, wishing and willing to fool the general public, professionals, the media and officials. The game becomes the energy. The game is the excitement and if done well, the game comes alive, never to die. Conspirators consider these pranks to be harmless. Their "jokes" are victimless forms of deception, they believe, where part of the thrill is seeing the hoax in print, or debated about on websites, as they watch their made-up tales or photo-shopped productions being argued about by people who should know better.

Who among us has not heard of the Loch Ness Monster named Nessie? It has been debated for years that the so-called "surgeon's photo" is not authentic. Bigfoot and the Patterson film is another high profile case of continued debate. Like a never-ending brick wall, reaching into the endless space above, dividing believer from non-believer and fact from fiction we built this wall choosing which side to stand on and have been unwilling or unable to leap from side to side. Debunkers may be debunking themselves as they take every known case and readily discard it. Perhaps it may be wise for a debunker to actually consider an event needs further investigation or state no comment at this time, rather than continually come out of the box with guns a blazing ready to shoot down any sighting or pick every testimony apart. Where does the line truly fall between debunkers and conspirators? In addition, on the other side of this brick wall, where do investigators and conspirators find separation? Are debunkers out there conjuring up weird tales to test the faithful, thus being conspirators? You bet they are! And are the so-called devoted researchers swallowing these tales, then adding selective data to an event and standing firm on their findings, thus being conspirators? You bet they are! A valued researcher sits on the wall overseeing and understanding both sides.

After all, why should Cryptozoology or the Paranormal be any different from the world around us? Did Lee Harvey Oswald act alone in the Kennedy assassination? Did the Apollo astronauts really land on the moon in 1969? Is the earth flat? And was there really a Holocaust in Europe? These questions may seem rather silly to many of us but how long have these debates raged? And how long have the facts, films and testimony of these events been examined and re-examined in an attempt in an attempt to either confirm of debunk them?

Now with this in mind, debating the Bigfoot Patterson film seems all too normal, pointless at this stage, but normal. As I have said many times, it really doesn't matter whether the Patterson film is authentic or not. If it's authentic, we'll search for Bigfoot and if it's a hoax --- we'll search for Bigfoot anyway."

## Four Steps Toward Becoming a Cryptozoology Field Researcher

Overanalyzing and speculating on cases, even going so far as to assume the sex life of Bigfoot or the unknown origins of Nessie at Loch Ness, as well as referring to obscure bits as puzzle pieces of evidence is as counterproductive as an armchair Cryptozoologist can dreadfully hope to become.

On the surface, it may appear constructive to many but the simple truth of the matter is it's a cheap, inexpensive, non-threatening, lazy way to promote another personal theory, entertain ones self or stir a debate rather than perform or initiate sound productive framework to get to the truth. Do not confuse evidence analyzes, documentation conformation and in-depth investigative research with the above-mentioned armchair tactics. Hours upon hours are wasted stating personal opinions via typed postings to internet sites and creating controversy over the same worn-out arguments. These are the arguments that will find no conclusion, change few minds and only continue the cycle of nonsensical chatter. Field research is a necessary tool. It's a tool that may be demanding, seemingly not very rewarding and more work than entertainment, but it's always productive. It's productive because experience, if nothing else, will be gained, and the fledgling researcher will begin to realize the value of honest, actual field work.

As uncomfortable as it may be for some to see these two words together ---- "Cryptozoology and Paranormal" ---- the fact is that many times, these paths do cross, not always by reality but often by interpretation. The mainstream of society sees little difference in the two and while education, explanation and future progress in both fields will certainly change this, for now, the connection exists. Too often, the general public will label sightings, encounters and events inappropriately, depending on who the teller of the story is, leaving the listener walking away not knowing if they just heard a ghost story, cryptid sighting or supernatural encounter. The teller may not believe in, or understand, Cryptozoology, hence transforming the event into a supernatural occurrence and/or vice versa. This fact needs to be addressed by the researcher and acknowledged. Simply tagging someone ignorant of the facts, or discounting a sighting, because the witness or a past researcher labeled it incorrectly, or misrepresented the data, will not gain progress in the field and bring us closer to the truth.

This condensed version of assisting the reader to become an active field researcher Cryptozoologist offers four fundamental steps, with the fourth being no less important than the first.

### Step One:
First is commitment and devotion. This sounds easy but it's not. However, these two attributes will carry you far no matter what interest in life you follow. Wilbur and Orville Wright had these qualities. Orville Wright

once wrote, "We were lucky enough to grow up in an environment where there was always much encouragement to children to pursue intellectual interests; to investigate whatever aroused curiosity." Neither of the Wright brothers ever received a high school diploma. Orville left high school to start a printing business and Wilbur stayed home to care for their ill mother. However, these two brothers had commitment and devotion and in a tiny little bike shop they built and flew the first airplane.

I have placed committment and devotion at the top of the steps because if these attributes are missing, none of the following steps are relevant.

### Step Two:

The second step is to self-education. Acquaint yourself with any topics you find of interest associated to Cryptozoology. Read Cryptozoological material, watch Cryptozoological-related television shows and search out Cryptozoological websites. Next, seek out seminars, courses and material, other than the obvious zoological studies, such as witness interviewing, photography, evidence collection methods and writing techniques.

Another course of direction, and one I find most valuable, is the hands-on approach. Became a zoo or animal shelter volunteer, camp out and hike as often as you can, study scouting and tracking, then test and improve your skills. Furthermore, when you go on a weekend excursion or take a vacation, research the area you're traveling to with a crypto-twist, the way that others may research restaurants, golf courses and hotel accommodations. Add to your list with past and present strange or cryptid sightings, area zoos and local legends. Researching such topic's these days is easy via the internet and toll free numbers. I cannot count the number of times I have called tourist information centers and have chatted with the desk clerk --- only to receive valuable information on the area's local legends or latest strange sightings.

Cryptozoological education may come in many forms, from a reliable book to field experience, or even simple conversation. I recall, many years ago, sitting and chatting with an old Indian about his hunting and trapping experiences. He talked all afternoon and late into the evening about tracking animals, being aware of their habits and recognizing unusual sounds. There were many things learned that day that have stuck with me throughout the years.

### Step Three:

One must get into the right mindset and maintain it. You are an investigator and researcher ---- speculation and assumptions must be erased from your vocabulary and performance, save for theoretic evaluation, which can should be done with extreme caution. Be prepared to defend and explain your theory yet never be close-minded to new evidence or fresh ideas.

Your theory (or ego) should not (and cannot) take precedence over a case, be it your investigation or someone else's. It is one thing to consider yourself thoroughly prepared and knowledgeable of a case yet quite another to be stubbornly single-minded or overly open-minded. Let the debaters, debate, let the hardcore skeptics debunk and the armchair crypto-theorists rant while you whistle your way through the woods, enjoying nature and obtaining evidence.

### Step Four:
The most important thing for any Cryptozoologist who wants to gather hard, authentic data is an "investigation protocol", which includes investigation supplies, construction of the case, case analysis, reporting and filing your case.

## Investigation Protocol

An investigation protocol begins by ignoring any assumptions. Leave your opinions separate from the case by clearly stating them as your opinions, never fact. Do not lead the witness, do not second guess the witness and never assume the more logical answer to be the correct answer. If an eyewitness states something like; "The thing seemed to fly, no, maybe just leaped.... yes, I think it was a leap." Take note of this witness' confusion, record it and take it into consideration when researching other similar cases.

### Four simply rules to follow when in the field:

1. **Document everything**
2. **Examine everything you can**
3. **Support your evidence**
4. **Record all testimony**

1.) Document everything ---- right down to the exact time of day and the weather. Many investigators seem to make the error of simply getting a witness' name, which many do not wish used anyway; an incomplete location, a basically useless date and a partial description of the event or sighting.

Witness information should include but is not limited to --- full name, age, sex, occupation, religious belief and education. For in-depth correctness and possible added insight, gather the eyewitness's state of mind and alertness, past experiences of the same or similar type, family history and even their theory of the event.

Location is relevant but seldom a clue of conclusion. Many times, the location actually hampers the investigation, assumptions crop up due to the simple placement of an event. For example, a Phantom Panther in a cemetery is at times automatically thought of as a spirit or ghost when in truth it may have been a real live animal. Don't fall into this trap.

Time may be one of the most useful pieces of documentation gathered. Do not stop at the obvious. Of course, record the complete date, but the time of day may reveal a secret, as would the length of the actual sighting time. The time of day may expose a pattern or even a reason behind the creature's movements, shadows cast and even the true ability to see clearly may hold explanations. The length of a sighting often transforms into Extended Time Claims, or E.T.C. Syndrome, much as is found in accident victims, where so much happened in such a short time the witness whole-heartily believes that minutes elapsed rather than seconds. This of course, in my opinion, adds truth to their statement.

A description of the event must be complete --- a hairy thing standing by the fence then vanishing tells little and ignores a lot. What was it doing, where was it looking, were any noises heard, any odors smelled, did it run, walk, leap, retreat or fly away? Find out exactly what it did look like and also ask for a sketch or sketch the varmint yourself as the eyewitness describes it.

2.) Examine everything, leaving no stone unturned. Take in the complete appearance of the location, even taking a couple of photographs. Make sure to use a scale system when photographing something, like measuring a weed the creature stood by or place an associate in the frame, etc. Check out the entire area for signs of activity or even the lack of activity. Take note of structures, foliage, waterways and vehicles, whatever is found at or by the scene, record it all.

3.) Support your Evidence. This is a big one! Look for area disturbance, same or like history, search the perimeter and when possible double document. Obtain police reports if possible or if they exist. If any personal injury or property damage was done, and the police were called, a police report must exist and is public record. If no report was filed with the local police still go visit the station to get an officer's name and statement. Even if that statement consists of the all too common remarks, "no comment" or "it wasn't reported", this will confirm your attempt.

When scanning an area do not simply look for beastly tracks, this means little. Debunkers use the lack of tracks found as an assumption nothing walked where the witness stated it did. I have gone to large shopping malls and not seen one human foot print but have noticed at least 2000 human beings shopping side by side. Look deeper, look for bent foliage, gnawed grass, hair, feathers, anything out of the ordinary.

The history of an entire location may reveal a lot. Now we are not just talking about local folklore, although this too needs investigated, but a more thorough history. Dig deeper by going to the library and/or web to find information about the location's past. Sometimes this simple search may add a lot to the understanding or support of the event.

Search the perimeter and visit the neighbors. Most are all too willing to tell their story. Some locals may reveal information that most investigators choose to ignore. I have gathered information about a pet panther living in the neighborhood while tracking a large dark puma sighting or heard about a petting zoo where wallabys had escaped, which explained a leaping animal in the woods.

A recent case I was called to in southeast Kentucky told of a phantom attacker terrorizing an elderly couple and made claims of a large winged figure standing on top of an old shed making strange bird-like sounds. Even a neighbor and daughter of the couple had seen the shed-figure on at least one late night occasion. When I personally inspected the rear of the shed I found markings of paint scrapped off the shed at about 7 feet high and an odd indentation in the ground 4 feet from the base of the shed. Looking further behind the structure, laying in some weeds, was a 2 by 10 board that matched the marks exactly when propped up against the rear wall. Climbing atop the shed, a Hershey's candy bar wrapper was found neatly tucked in the rain gutter. Then I scanned the area below and could see a path through the tall weeds that led to another house. Following the path revealed a rather large teenage boy, who admitted to the prank and even showed me his cape and a broken duck call that made a unique, piercing sound. When asked why the teen did it, he stated, "I was bored." The moral of this story, "Check out the complete perimeter."

Double document, take notes and photographs, tape record if allowed and know how to retrieve a good plaster cast when possible. Speak to all of the witnesses, individually if feasible, and search for other witnesses. Then re-interview the witnesses months, or even years, later. Many times this type of updating may reveal a hoax or add important testimony that escaped the witness at the time of the incident. Other advantages to the re-interview may give the researcher added information or verification of the event. Unlike lightning, these odd encounters do seem to strike the same individuals twice.

Supporting evidence takes many forms, as does non-supporting evidence. As simple and obvious as this statement is on the surface, it finds many experts and witnesses perplexed as to what supporting evidence truly is. But first let's look at what non-supporting evidence is, thus answering two questions with this one line of thought.

Non-supporting evidence encompasses all assumptions. Evidence is not items brought forward with thoughts that it must fit. It is not a method of elimination, thus arriving at a conclusion. No, in the world of the unexplained, negatives cannot add to positives. Example: seeing an unknown creature that does not look like a dog, cat, rabbit or squirrel does not add up to a Cryptid, yet this is how many witnesses sum it up. Be very careful before leaping from the known to the extreme unknown.

Another error often noticed are non-supporting pieces evidence tagged "exhibit A" that are about as related to the event as my left sock. These exhibits usual include, but are not limited to, such things as folklore, dreams, legends and even commercial products claimed as evidence. Yes, you read that correctly ---- commercial products. These old photos or sketches brought forth as evidence to support sightings or strange encounters with an unknown history and no knowledge of its origin or maker are absurd. Science is not about guesswork. This is theory and should be clearly stated as such.

4.) Record all Testimony ---- Never count on your memory. Write it down or better yet, tape record it at the time or at the very least, as you are leaving the scene. Do not rule out anyone's testimony at any time, even if it does not seem to fit. And do not add or subtract from a testimony ---- ever! Do not coach or lead the witness. Let the witness speak and describe events in their terms, at their pace. Your job is only to record and clarify. Besides gathering basic information, the testimony when studied may hold secrets to a pattern, flap, or reveal a hoax.

Taking the latter first, try to never be sucked in by a tantalizing tale even if it is interesting, supportive of your own personal research or the witnesses seem to be genuine. Check it all out. It will be you who will have to explain each and every aspect of the case, including parts you may have left out and the reasons for those oversights. Let us take an example I received in my e-mail and see how many errors or false statements you find in the following story.

## *Hoax Example:*

It was mid-winter, Saturday December 30, 1983 around 7:33 p.m. just south of St. Louis, Missouri when four young people came upon an injured thing they could only imagine was Momo, the Missouri Bigfoot. The two couples, Robert and Jennifer and Michael and Connie were driving along route 94. It was clear weather and dusk was just settling onto the countryside.

Robert was out showing off his dad's 1991 Dodge Viper when just before crossing the Mason City Bridge, a large hairy creature laying along the road was spotted by Jennifer. Screaming out in terror, Jennifer demanded Michael pull over and the youths approached the injured beast. Robert, fearing for their safety, grabbed a large stick. Moaning was now heard, even as traffic roared past. Michael held tight onto Connie's hand but did not get any closer than 10 yards from the animal. Scared but curious, Robert and Jennifer continued their march toward the creature.

Robert could now see a dead animal grasped in the right hand of the thing they called Momo. They assumed it had gone after road kill and was hit by a passing vehicle. The thing was bleeding profusely. Jennifer insisted Robert help the creature but he refused. Michael, being a brave soul, flipped the beast onto its back and confirmed this was indeed the elusive Momo. Wright County sheriff's deputies soon showed up and took over the scene, demanding that the group leave.

Thought this story may interest you!
Signed, David T.

At least 14 obviously wrong, or questionable, statements are in this one account.

1. December the 30th, 1983 was a Friday not Saturday.
2. Why did the youths immediately jump to the conclusion it was Momo at first sight?
3. Route 94 is west of St. Louis, not south.
4. At 7:33 p.m. during a Midwestern winter, it would be very dark not dusk.
5. Dodge Vipers first came out in 1992 not '91 and they are two seaters so 4 youths could not be in the automobile. In addition, they would not be released for nine years after this event supposedly took place.
6. Mason City does not have a bridge and is west of St. Louis, not south.
7. Robert was showing off the car so why did Jennifer demand Michael to pull over?
8. The traffic continued to go past, with 4 youths and a large beast by the road?

9. The beast was badly injured but managed to hold onto the road kill?
10. Michael and Connie didn't get any closer than 10 yards yet Michael turned the beast over?
11. Wright County is far south and west of the area.
13. Why were no last names used?
14. Why no police officer's names used and why would the police demand the couples to leave?

In addition, no information was given of the sender, other than David T. This leaves nothing to check into and no way to interview any of the witnesses to the story.

(Sadly this is one of the better-hoaxed letters, I've received.)

## Pattern Reporting

Pattern reporting often occurs when researchers attempt to create something that is not truly there. It also happens when another researcher picks up a collection of reports that come from the first researcher's "hometown region" and assume that it shows a pattern of sightings in a small area. In truth, this is just the researcher "writing what he knows", which tends to make his immediate area look more active than other areas. This is not something that is done to be misleading but is actually thorough coverage of the immediate area.

However, selective data, regional interviews and limited sources used can all create a false pattern of encounters. Even old encounters retold, adding new undocumented twists, can on the surface appear as a legitimate investigation but a close examination will often find little to verify and less to aid in the creature's identification. Your hope, your agenda, your purpose must be to maintain a high level of creditability. Understand, pattern reporting is created by the researcher, not the witness.

Case examination, scrutiny and questioning is not a way of debunking the case. It's easy for some to immediately scoff at legitimate cross-examination, which is not debunking, but rather the basic foundation of scientific research methods and principle. For many years, I have pointed out this false "building of a brick wall" by pattern reporting. One must take away the possible exaggerations, consider the hype, ignore the media conclusions and be guarded when listening to "experts'" theories that link one case to another. Furthermore, one must take into consideration the regional beliefs as well as the labeling of an event. Once this evaluation is carefully examined, all of a sudden we're looking at a much simpler encounter, no matter how unique a single source assumes it to be.

Excellent examples of this are the Mothman and Jersey Devil cases. In both of these cases I believe something was encountered originally and I believe the eyewitnesses believed they saw something strange but it's the researchers "add-on's" and transformations that make these creatures change from a probable migrating rare crane or deformed child to an unknown supernatural creature.

Be sure to avoid pattern reporting. Build yourself a network of researchers. E-mailing, snail mail and telephone them periodically for other regional reports and insight. Don't fall into the trap of regional assumptions and false associations that many lone researchers condemn themselves to.

## Flaps

The basic definition of a "flap" is a grouping of related sightings or events that occur over a specific, or even a very wide, area. This is, however, different from pattern reporting. With a flap, it is a series of sightings that is created by reports from witnesses and not a series put together by the researcher. It may be a flap of any abnormal event from Bigfoot sightings to UFO reports. These flaps might last for days, weeks or even months. They can cross state lines or at times be found worldwide. In fact, at this writing there is a 'flap' of Black Panther sightings being reported in the United States, England, France and Australia.

A flap is jointly, and perhaps equally due, to a number of reasons. First a heightened awareness for the strange event or critter, where looking for, seeing and / or believing it was seen makes it a reality or indeed is a reality. In this type of situation, we will have some possible legitimate sightings and scores of misidentifications. Could it be that flaps of sightings are nothing more than the public becoming temporarily aware of such encounters and creating a localized mass hysteria?

Secondly, it may be an acceptance to report the encounter, where the witness now believes he or she will not be ignored or be branded a fool. This also occurs with crime reporting too, especially in rape or child molestation cases. Once someone comes forward, others often follow. The same may apply to corporate crime, when once exposed, we all look a little harder.

Third, a slow news day may be responsible or it may be that a news reporter has done his homework and actually follows up on a case. Not too often, is a good reporter talked about but they are out there and they are fighting for their story, their interests and even answers. However, the public buys the papers and sees one sighting as news, two sightings as bigger news and three sightings becoming old news. Then, throw in the mix a few hoaxes, pranksters and gotta-see-my-name-in-print freaks and things start to spin out of control. Soon the entire event becomes a circus with people selling t-shirts, waving signs and loading shotguns.

In the Lawndale, Illinois Thunderbird case, "Texas John Huffer" (alleged, self-proclaimed Algonquin Indian Chief) was, and is, our 't-shirt salesmen', still peddling a film of turkey vultures that was taken miles and days away from the original incident.

If we were to assume a flap of sightings has credibility in Cryptozoology, it would be wise to consider the possibilities that the cryptid reportedly seen must fall into one of these following categories: migration, expanding territories, injury, disorientation, loss of habitation or nature's natural force.

## Nature's Natural Force

A leading cause of cryptid sightings, and the flaps that follow, might very well be as simple of an explanation as nature. At the turn of the millennium, I theorized about weather changes, storms, forest fires and other natural disasters in relationship to cryptid reports and soon set out to prove the theory or at least show cause that such a theory should be seriously considered.

The study to support cryptid reports because of "nature's natural force" gathered documented weather data and compared it to cryptid witness testimonies. It showed that in the weeks immediately following a disaster, cryptid sightings within a 1000 mile radius raised dramatically turning into 'flaps', media events and at times, even cases where newly named cryptids were born. I believe when one closely looks at this correlation between nature's natural force, misidentification and y-creatures are the likely culprits to explain the flaps.

Tornado's, hurricanes, snow blizzards, ice storms, forest fires and floods devastate property, humans, live stock and wild animal populations, many times in an unprecedented flash. These natural disasters pick up, move, transform, reorganize and change the face and the value of the land. Wild animals must cope and they must quickly adjust or perish. It's during this window of adjustment that survival outweighs risk and stealth. Food supplies are lost and once safe surroundings are now dangerous places that lead to unknown paths and many times, into human territory. It's a metaphoric bridge that must be crossed as the animal refugees search for a new and safe haven.

Sighting data, when compared to weather statistics, strongly suggests a solid correlation exists between multiple cryptid reports and harsh weather conditions. Data revealed that areas that are hardest hit by "perfect storms" are then followed and subject to cryptid reports. It is my contention that these cryptid flaps are due to, and caused by, these natural conditions. Three causes exist. First are the known wild animals that are rarely seen and are reported by the novice as misidentifications. Second are exotic pets that have escaped from weather-caused destruction, thus contributing to the reported cryptid. Finally, if any area unknowns do exist, then actual cryptids would be on the move and seen when, as in the first two cases, conditions cause these animals to be seen when they normally would not be.

When a cryptid or y-creature has been reported in close time approximation to harsh weather conditions, one cannot merely consider the immediate area. I surmise a hurricane hitting the Florida coast in June may yield a cryptid or mystery animal report in July from Mississippi or even further away. Documentation exists that collared and monitored cougars have covered more than 1,000 miles in a few week period from their original territory and have traveled right past, or even through, heavily human populated cities. Furthermore, bears have also been documented traveling over 1,000 miles in a relatively short time. And who has not heard the cases of lost family pets that struggle their way home over thousands of miles of unknown terrain? The documentation exists that animals are capable of amazing feats, successfully enduring hundreds of miles of unknown area.

When it comes to tornados, an F-2 is considered a significant tornado, this rating signifies winds of a 113 to 157 mph. These winds are strong enough to rip the roof off a frame-built home and are capable of snapping or uprooting a good-sized tree. How potentially damaging would heavy winds be to a den, lean-to, nest or food supply? How much havoc, and how drastic of a landscape facelift, might a fierce storm or flash flood cause, transforming a once safe and secure environment into something completely alien to the animal that once dwelled there?

If we look at the 1977 Flap of Thunderbird sightings reported across Illinois and start with the first and most documented case at Lawndale, Illinois in Logan County, then something weather related jumps right out at you. In late May 1977, only weeks before the first report of two Thunderbirds invading the Illinois skies and allegedly picking up Marlon Lowe, an F-4 tornado hit Logan County, Illinois. Tornado data from 1951 to 1995 shows that no F-4 tornado had ever hit Logan County except for the May 1977 twister. An F-4 tornado intensity phase is devastating. It brings with it wind speeds of 207 to 260 mph and can level well-constructed houses and throw cars about as if they were toys.

From here, let's leap to the continued reported sightings of the big birds in and around Lake Shelbyville in Shelby County, Illinois. This is the location Texas John Huffer filmed what he and some others believe to be thunderbirds. In late August 1977, an F-3 tornado tore through the county, and as in Logan County, it strangely was the strongest tornado on record for Shelby county. An F-3 can overturn trains and even uproot trees. Its winds may reach 158 to 206 mph. This Shelby County tornado might have been all it took to keep these large birds on the move and perhaps even disoriented or off course, thus exposing themselves to the countless witnesses who reported the birds for the remainder of 1977. Some researchers now theorize they were on a flight back to the southern hemisphere.

The few decades of reports now available simply don't include enough twisters to permit a reliable analysis of the nation's tornado risk. Therefore, meteorologists such as Harold E. Brooks of the National Severe Storms Laboratory in Norman, have turned to computer simulations. In their most recent study, Brooks and his colleagues started with weather and damage data from 10,000 tornadoes that occurred between 1921 and 1995. Using just five parameters, their simulation generated a realistic mix of 4 million tornadoes over 30,000 years that the team then subjected to statistical analyses.

Southeastern Oklahoma fared worst in the simulation, with each point in the area getting hit once every 4,000 years on average. A large portion of the central United States—stretching from the Colorado-Kansas border to western North Carolina and from the Gulf Coast to southern Minnesota—suffered a twister approximately once every 10,000 years. Nevada suffered tornadoes so infrequently that data points to the possibility that they might get damaged only once every 5 million years. So, beginning with the obvious and considering only tornado verses cryptid stats --- Oklahoma should logs hundreds of cryptid encounters where as Nevada's cryptid encounters should be basically non-existent.

Most recently, Hurricane Katrina started out modestly on August 23, 2005 in the Bahamas as a tropical wave that emerged from the remnants of a tropical depression that had been in the Caribbean. It gradually grew into the season's 11th named storm and the fourth hurricane to make landfall in South Florida with maximum sustained winds of 80 mph and gusts up to 95 mph. After quickly crossing Southern Florida, Katrina emerged again over water in the Southeastern Gulf of Mexico near the Florida Keys, and strengthened to the 2005 season's third major hurricane before reorganizing into the most powerful storm in the Central Gulf since Hurricane Camille and third category five hurricane in as many years with winds as high as 175 mph. It became the fourth most powerful hurricane of all time.

After coming ashore as a category one hurricane in South Florida, Katrina struck two more times along the Gulf Coast. First in Buras, Louisiana with 140 mph winds and then near Bay St. Louis, Mississippi with 135 mph winds. It created a 27 foot storm surge in Gulfport, Mississippi and a 22 foot storm surge in Bay St. Louis. Winds as high as 90 mph were felt as far east as Mobile, Alabama, which experienced its worst flooding in 90 years. Waves as high as 48 feet happened offshore in the Gulf of Mexico. Some 50 people were killed in coastal Mississippi, including 30 in an apartment complex in Biloxi. Katrina even ripped off part of the roof of the Louisiana Superdome, where 10,000 people were staying in the facility, which was being used as a shelter of last resort. Extensive flooding occurred in New Orleans, which was actually spared the brunt of the storm. The 9th ward in the Crescent City was under water, as well as 80 percent of the city. People fled to their attics to escape drowning and some were rescued by helicopters and boats. At this writing, the latest death toll is at 508 and still counting, with damage estimates ranging from $20 billion to $50 billion dollars.

Cryptozoological reports have soared in Katrina's wake: Out of place (y-creature) alligators have been reported by the media in Arkansas and Kentucky, Alabama hunters have allegedly seen and photographed a cougar, Florida Skunk Ape reports have been on the rise and Tennessee, Virginia and West Virginia bird watchers claim rare sightings of Gulf bird species in their own 'backyards'.

To summarize nature's natural force vs. cryptid sightings, one can logically determine and quickly confirm supporting data. This theory illustrates possibilities that reach beyond animal misidentifications and are more feasible than roaming bands of cryptids. If a tornado or hurricane can place a car in a tree, could it not do the same to a now dead deer? If extreme flooding can wash a building away, could not a beast in the path find itself in an entirely different environment? And if forest fires drive out bears couldn't Bigfoot sightings manifest....? Interesting questions indeed.

## Investigation Supplies

Now that we have covered the basic steps of what to do --- and what not to do --- we should discuss what tools should be used in your investigations. I learned early on to keep my bag packed and at the ready. Often times, reports of sightings and encounters, or even rumors of strange occurrences, come at the most unexpected times and in the least expected places. Time becomes an important factor. Clues such as footprints or eyewitnesses still on the scene might be lost if you do not, or cannot, act immediately. Of course, another reason to be prepared for the next investigation demands that the least of your concerns should be getting your "stuff" together. Not only will this delay you and mentally sidetrack you, but most importantly, you may forget an essential "tool". Its essential that you keep your items packed and at the ready because when trying to document a Cryptozoological event, professional procedure is a must. Cryptozoology certainly does not need another, "the one that got away story" because you forgot the back-up batteries.

The unexplained can be a strange game. How many times have you purchased a different car and then suddenly you start to notice how many of that same model are already on the road? Cosmic games seem to follow these same rules. Once you have prepared yourself, opening the door of possibility, and prepared yourself to document such things ---- a completely new horizon is experienced. Preparation is 80% of the game.

### General items needed:

1. A good strong, watertight carrying case. It should be something you can throw around and have no concerns as to environmental changes. To determine size needed, place all your supplies in front of you before purchasing a case.

2. Recording instruments, e.g. pencils, notepads, voice tape recorder, 2 cameras, and extra batteries (still factory sealed). I leave the camcorder in the car and laptop at home. This makes most witnesses nervous and distracts you from a good, solid search and interview. Obviously, do not pack loose ink pens or loose batteries.

3. Night vision, listening devices and trip cameras --- once considered expensive high tech-equipment now can be purchased at a very reasonable cost and the field value far exceeds the investment. A great starting point would be to browse through a outdoor gear catalog. You can find just about anythign you would need here.

### Next are the basic field tools:

1. Pack a good 25-foot tape measure.
2. An average-sized flashlight and small pen light for a back up.
3. A decent pair of binoculars will be satisfactory for your needs.
4. An up-to-date atlas and other local maps, if appropriate, as well as a quality compass.
5. A small pocketknife may be needed to collect samples.
6. Baggies and an air tight sealing small jar.
7. Dental Stone for casting tracks (keep it separate from the main bag).
8. At least 20 feet of strong rope (if you do not bring it, you will need it).
9. Guidebooks relevant to your needs.
10. Florescent spray paint (for extreme emergencies, ie. marking your path, writing rescue messages.)

Personal items are a must and often times overlooked. I cannot stress the need for a change of clothes that should included in your investigation bag. Trekking through knee-deep mud, crawling under a filthy porch, ripping pants on a barbed wire fence are but a few of the nasty experiences I have had. That's not to mention the time I dripped mustard on my shirt and had to return to an interview I was doing. If not for a change of clothes, I think the witness may have thought I was less than professional. Other personal items should include a little bit of money for tolls, phone calls (if the cell phone is out of range), snacks or even to buy your witness a cup of coffee. This polite gesture can go a long way.

Once the checklist is complete and the bag is packed, set up a scheduled time, every three months should do, to inventory and confirm everything is still ready and in working order.

## *Construction of the Case*

After the initial field investigation is complete, sort out the evidence, organize the documentation and compare other events in your files to this occurrence. Think of different ways you could corroborate or invalidate certain issues or events through personally field testing them. For instance, if ghostly balls of light or glowing eyes are seen in a cemetery each night after midnight, go there yourself at the event's testified time and look around. Take note of each angle you could approach the source, eliminate every possible reflection, then photograph the scene whether or not, as in this case, the ghostly ball of light or eyes are seen or not.

Your next step may be to contact a trusted colleague to "tap their mind" as to authenticity, hoaxers, past documentation and/or theories of the event at hand. Here, caution should be heeded. The key word is "trusted" colleague. Some investigators have learned to take a story and run with it, adding a quick insert and telephone or e-mail to the witness ---- just enough to claim it as their own research. This has happened to me more times than I wish to think about it.

Another troubling issue we should address is the over usage of pseudonyms (a name other than ones own, assumed for some purpose) within a given testimony of the paranormal event or creature sighting. What these purpose is for a "changed name" should be asked and then explained by the witness. Some reasons are obvious ---- ridicule, harassment, privacy and community status but there are other motives as well, including one that is rarely mentioned. That motive is the investigator's personal agenda. In some cases, the investigator himself may in fact make up a person's name for numerous reasons. First, and worst, was that the entire occurrence was a fabrication. Secondly, the event was actually witnessed by the investigator himself, and then a pseudonym was added for realism and appearance of a true and separate investigation. Another possible motive may be that the investigator wishes to keep the story for himself, thus leaving others at a dead end and forced to seek information from the original investigator. The most prevalent motive investigators may have for name changing is the lawsuit craze that has swept the country. With that in mind, it may be that the use of a pseudonym may be something more often done by the investigator, rather than the witness. I would strongly suggest to anyone inserting a pseudonym to add a quick, simple explanation for the purpose or at the very least acknowledge it was done. Many times the acknowledgement alone uncloaks the obvious reason.

Watch out how you label something or what you associate it with while building your case. Too often, a Homo Anomalous (human-like creature, usually hairy, walking upright) is intermixed with UFO sightings. Now this is not to say this "UFO-Foot" theory is right or wrong. Labeling it should be stated  that it is for organization never, ever for absolute conclusion. An orb (sphere ball of energy) may be far removed from ghosts and spirits yet this is now the popular and entertaining belief. In reference to orb's I lean toward self-strength, excitement and energy found within each of us or simply a lousy photo.

Once the case is well under-construction, realize this, it will remain under-construction. Even if years later the case is revealed as an out and out hoax, other factors have now taken over. One of those factors may include a "cult following" and an undying belief in the event. Another factor I have seen is one or more researchers, unrelated to the original investigation, have now "picked it up". Perhaps they did a similar investigation and now use your case as yet another piece of evidence to support their research or theories and are unwilling to let it go. Even choosing not to accept any new evidence brings demise to the case. Folklore may also play a role in the continuance of the event with locals retelling the story, adding incredible, outlandish statements as fact. The case then mutates from an unexplained event to a case of controversy or a campfire tale of terror.

On the other hand, if your case does survive the test of time, and the skeptic's attacks, and the ridicule it is guaranteed to receive, the status of "under-construction", will remain. Never is the term "the end" found in unexplained events. The researcher must keep this in mind, which makes the need for a complete and thorough documentation even more important.

## Case Analysis

This can be a tricky area for investigators to enter into and some choose not to do so, while others refuse to accept those who do. I find case analysis not only to be acceptable but also expected. I personally question a researcher that has no opinion or deliberately throws out a quick cryptic statement or worn out cliché to conclude the event. One must question why these people are not open or receptive to other's impressions?

 Case analysis can be a valuable tool used to stimulate thought or at the least, very interesting and entertaining.

When analyzing your case, or someone else's case, cover all the angles you can but keep in mind that "unknown" or "unexplained" means just that. An unexplained event is not going to be explained while sitting at the keyboard and an unknown sighting is not going to become known while staring at a witness' sketch. Many hoaxes, pranks and honest errors may be revealed during a field investigation or during personal interviews. Theories are a part of the analysis however and can be conjured up anywhere at anytime, although it's best that a theory be scientifically created and first shared with trusted colleagues for added insight and credibility.

Analyzing a case with other than actual evidence is found by reaching for conclusions, creating theories, making assumptions and constructing opinions. When using these methods remember this, one or more reasons may exist for the event. Once while on an investigation, witnesses told of a shadowy figure that would appear in the fall accompanied by high-pitched whistles. As I "camped" out on location at the testified time and from the angle of the eyewitnesses a strange shadow indeed appeared, at times coupled with a high screeching almost bird-like sound. Walking toward the sound, the whistles were discovered to be coming from the wind whipping down a streetlight's guideline warning tube only 6 feet from where the shadow would appear. Turning around, it was soon revealed the shadow was from a waving Halloween flag that was being reflected off a large plate glass window. The relfection occurred when the wind moved the flag, tripping the outdoor motion light, thus created the movement, shadow and sound at the same time.

Another item to be wary of is the notion that "all angles have been covered", falsely leading one to a believe that this is what it must be! Here all one needs to remember is this --- how often have you heard someone say while looking for their lost keys or wallet, "I can't find it and I've looked everywhere!"? Well, obviously, they have not looked everywhere or they would have found the lost item. Do not ever assume you have covered all the angles to an unknown event unless you find the answer to the mystery!

## Reporting the Case

This may be the most unrewarding and difficult part of your case development. More times than not, cases are only kept alive by the witness themselves or the field investigator, at least in the early stages. News agencies may find room for the unusual if it is close to Halloween or if numerous sighting occur. Television generally has interest in the story only if film accompanies the tale and police, game wardens and other officials may listen, but seldom seriously investigate or document a report. If you do choose to report it to a game warden, or the police, be prepared to receive the run around. Usually quick short replies, standard answers and/or instructions for you to contact a different office will be in response to your report.

Choose your methods wisely and make sure you have permission from all parties involved, before naming names or taking photographs. This can-include, but is not limited to, the witnesses, landowners and any sources or interviews conducted. Once you have started the reporting of your case, there is no turning back. Make sure all your ducks are all in a row, so to speak, at least as best as you feel they can be. Try to contact and report the case to as many sources as you can at one time. This may require scores of phone calls and numerous e-mails but is worth the effort.

In this field, even the reporting and contacting will become part of the case, so document all of it, even the e-mails not returned or the phone calls that kept you going from one department to the next.

## Filing the Case

This is a very important step and it must be done correctly because, as stated earlier, your case will remain under-construction for all time. Make sure everything is together: evidence stored, well documented, photographs protected and original notes saved. Label your case what it is, not what you think it is or what the witness thought it was. For instance, a shadow crossing a yard in Atlanta is not a ghost, nor is it a Bigfoot or panther. It is a shadow, so file it under "shadow" or something similar to the actual event.

Often the mistake of trying to file any given case is found in the classification of it, so try to stay away from exact identification and personally associated locations.

Taking the latter first is the "Investigator factor" when many documented events can be sourced back to a Cryptozoologist of that region, not all, but many. Speaking for myself, many of the sightings of phantom panthers, for instance, would have fallen through the cracks in my region if I had not started documenting them. This too may be the case in many other locations with other interested parties. Another problem is that Bigfooters tend to label any, or most, Homo Anomalous sightings as Bigfoots. If a UFO researcher lives in a given area, you may see more strange beasts related to UFO's and not thought of as cryptids. Please keep in mind these are examples.

Still yet another problem is the labeling, who is doing it and with what mindset? Is a beast in the cemetery a ghost or a neighborhood dog? Is a black panther in the yard a spirit or a cryptid or perhaps just kids at play? We simply need to organize things without any conclusion in mind. Remember that a true pattern may surface due to our own ability to investigate these occurrences in an unbiased manner.

# 8. CRYTIDS: FACT OR FANTASY?
## With Deborah Shira

**W**hat are Cryptids?

The short, direct answer is ---- Cryptids are animals unclassified by Western science.

However, this seemingly simple question, and its answer, is hotly debated not only among those who openly admit their ignorance of the term butis also heatedly debated amongst those who have devoted a great deal of time, study and effort to the field of Cryptozoology. An explanation of an unknown animal in the mind of a wild-eyed researcher may be twisted into a cryptid as a new undiscovered species, simply by theorizing on a single sighting or testimony and ignoring present testimony from investigators who physically researched the event and who have found the event to hold no more evidence than a misidentified known species. It is wise to tread lightly on these claims and accounts from known dramatic-minded researchers or overzealous witnesses.

Are mythological beasts that have astonishing appearances or do uncharacteristic things correctly classified as cryptids? The answer to this is a simple "no". Fire-breathing dragons, Pegasus the flying horse, the serpentine Nagas, the animal-featured Yalli and the elephant-faced crocodiles called Makaras, to name a few, are not cryptids. They are as the term implies, "mythological beasts". Although some may argue that from most of these legendary creatures, slivers of true animals were described but this is "evidence" best filed away and not seriously sought.

Can the extinct dinosaurs, and other thought to be extinct beasts, be cryptids? Again, this answer is obviously, "no". Known extinct animals from Tyrannosaur Rex to the Wooly Mammoth are not cryptids. Many might take issue with this broad statement but some kind of proof must exist before moving a known extinct beast to the other side of the line. Claims that these animlas still exist are too often based on a couple of questionable testimonies or half-baked theories. One of the best examples of a thought to be extinct animal that is still actively sought, and justly so, is the Thylacine of Australia, also referred to as the Tasmanian wolf or Tasmanian tiger. However, the Thylacine is not a cryptid but rather a known beast that Cryptozoologists still seek.

Bernard Heuvelmans, the generally accepted "Father of Cryptozoology," and man who coined the term "Cryptozoology" once wrote:

*"Admittedly, a definition need not conform necessarily to the exact etymology of a word. But it is always preferable when it really does so which I carefully endeavored to achieve when I coined the term `cryptozoology`. All the same being a very tolerant person, even in the strict realm of science, I have never prevented anybody from creating new disciplines of zoology quite distinct from cryptozoology. How could I, in any case?"So, let people who are interested in founding a science of `unexpected animals`, feel free to do so, and if they have a smattering of Greek and are not repelled by jaw breakers they may call it` aprosbletozoology` or `apronoeozoology` or even `anelistozoology`. Let those who would rather be searching for `bizarre animals` create a `paradoozoology`, and those who prefer to go a hunting for `monstrous animals`, or just plain `monsters`, buildupa `teratozoology `ormoresimplya `pelorology `.*

*"But for heavens sake, let cryptozoology be what it is, and what I meant it to be when I gave it its name over thirty years ago!"*

Today, the once understood term "Cryptozoology" and the later created word "Cryptid", have taken on a much larger blanket of understanding and one that wrongly covers the widely misunderstood definition. Mr. Heuvelmans would not be pleased.

Granted, the term cryptid does mean different things to different people, including those who lay claim to the title of Cryptozoologist. For example, if an unknown animal (cryptid) in the forest is later captured, which would either reveal it as a known species or create another, then it is no longer 'hidden' and no longer classified as a cryptid. Y-Creatures (why are they there? type of critters) or otherwise known as out-of-place creatures (oop), too often wrongly fall into this category. Being first thought of as cryptid, soon are recognized as known species. Another misconception of a cryptid is an animal that has been found to be more paranormal or folklore-like than factual. Some examples of this can be found in the stories of Mothman, the Jersey Devil and Demon Black Dogs. Although, I do not discard these claims, I do not think of them as cryptids but rather chose to examine the testimony and leave the debate to others.

A good example of an animal that is sighted often but finds itself in a state of "cryptid limbo", would be the Mysterious Black Panthers. Are they misidentifications, released or escaped pets, phantoms or falsehoods? If these are, as I believe some encounters to be, Eastern cougars or a subspecies of hidden pockets of unknown large cats with breeding population's possibly creating hybrids, then cryptids they may be. But mystery sightings walk a thin line to cryptids. It would be better stated for Cryptozoology as a whole to take a closer look at the creatures, testimonies, evidence and history before adding another "Beaver-eater" named critter to this ever-growing list.

But back to the basics.... Is Cryptozoology and it's search for Cryptids a form of science or entertainment? Is Cryptozoology fact or fiction, documentation or speculation? In order to transform an outlandish claim of a cryptid into a documented, scientifically classified animal requires undeniably solid proof; i.e.: a specimen, nothing less.

## Creation of the Cryptid Confirmation Commitee (CCC)

Creating a Cryptid Confirmation Committee was initially hoped to be an elementary procedure. Years of concern stemmed from witnessing the public's lack of understanding as to what exactly cryptids are brought solicitude involving months of research. However, before disclosing my plan publicly, I intensely monitored the lack of uniformity found in the term cryptid and the ease in which another single sighting or undocumented story was added to this ever growing list of cryptids. These unscientific cryptid acceptances confirmed the need to design an organization with standard guidelines and seek out a volunteer team of Cryptozoology buffs and experts, whose only "committee concern", would be to vote on or off suggested unclassified animals, thus creating a recognized list.

However, this was to become nothing short of a true challenge, thankfully, first to come on board for this all-important project was Deborah Kaye Shira.

Deborah Kaye Shira was born in 1955 in Pittsburgh, Pennsylvania. Deborah's father was a career Navy man and her mother a true Southern lady. Deborah was exposed at a very young age to the adventures of moving to new places and the vast accumulation of knowledge along the way. This was to set the foundation that would establish the love of travel and need to acquire all forms of knowledge that she lives by to this day, without deviation. A firm believer in the saying, "Where there is smoke, there is fire", Deborah would wonder about the possibilities of strange creatures existing.

Very quickly thereafter, a sighting of Bigfoot on the news opened the world of Cryptozoology to her. Deborah attained seven minor degrees in subjects as diverse as Physics, Chemistry, Geology, Astronomy, Theology, Calculus and Statistics, and Medical Technology. She continues to take college classes as the interest in a field of research occurs, but no longer seeks the degrees, which to her are only pieces of paper and the extraneous classes needed to obtain them are only to line the college coffers. The love of travel, knowledge, and cryptids remains an innate part of her life. As to cryptids and cryptozoology, she continues to work to legitimatize the science through the elimination of superstitious ignorance, the inclusion of myths and legends, and the unconscionable efforts of those "Cryptozoologists" who wish to keep an aura of mystery and the surreal around the science in an effort to line their own pockets. Deborah's interest, knowledge and education in the field of Cryptozoology is well known and respected, not only at the Cryptozoology website's she frequents but in her hometown community circles as well. Deborah was a valuable resource the CCC needed to go from a simple conception to a solid reality.

Hours, days turning into weeks, then months passed as Deborah and I researched and created the requirements for CCC. Creating procedures, committee protocol, voting forms and research guidelines first took a backseat to finding an accepted, basic definition of a cryptid. Finding no definition from reliable sources or finding definitions of the term cryptid that were so vague in nature they could be, and have been, turned, twisted and manipulated as arguments to fit any strange, out of place or unknown beast, the decision was then made to create our own definition, fine-tuned for everyone to use and understand.

This first group of volunteers would find a most difficult task awaiting them. After a democratically accepted list of cryptids would be established, any future committee volunteers would then be more involved in reviews rather than adding new evidence to support yet another cryptid. This committee's objective was not to pick out or chose a list of cryptids, then discard the others. It is a pyramid list with the most probable cryptids at the top. A confirmation, with an added heightened awareness, of the few cryptids our team of experienced, devoted researchers documented would place high on the most likely to be discovered list ---- a "ten most wanted" list, if you will. Sounds easy enough, yes? Nope, not at all.

Much concern and many ideas have branched from each thought into ten new and old concerns. There were discussions early on for the creation of not only the formation and duties of the committee member's but also involving the deployment of the organization's volunteers. There was further development of the guidelines, rules, voting procedures, timetables, and even the essential complex tasks of cryptid definition and sorting through the chaos of existing cryptid lists, witnesses, locations, evidence and reports of cryptids, that others carelessly stacked together. All this had to be considered and ironed out before even the first vote was to be cast on a cryptid.

So, creating and gathering a team is what we set out to do for the purpose and validity of the cryptids claimed to exist. This was not to draw a hard line in the sand, dividing unknown sightings or to arbitrarily expel testimony of encounters, but rather a "standard yardstick" if you will, that future Cryptozoologists can look to with supporting evidence and make a creature "more likely" to be a cryptid than the next.

Personally I cannot blindly or totally accept Cryptozoology's cryptids. The past "experts" continue to haphazardly create, or suggest to the world, where the line is between what is a cryptid and what is not --- such creatures as Bigfoots are cryptids, but Road Trolls are not, Nessie at Loch Ness is but the Jersey Devil is not. The definitions they have created truly amaze me. If an unknown creature is explainable, even in their terms as a cryptid, then it must be one. But add a hoof here, a wing there and a hoax, prank, urban legend or supernatural tale it is transformed. When you filter out the exaggeration, knock off the media's hype and evaluate the witness, a clearer picture often develops. My personal opinions rule out many creatures as ever being "real".

Cryptid lists were found with as few as 86 strange, weird beasts (mostly mythological) on a list, while other lists ranged as high as having 747 cryptids --- most of which were missing pertinent data. These cryptid lists included undocumented evidence, numerous unreliable sources (a few based on blurry photographs) and even creatures once told around campfires, and then forgotten. The truth is that these "thrown-together cryptid lists" have sadly became the norm of our early research instead of the exception. It was more obvious than ever that something had to be done and done systematically to stop this runaway train but ahead of us was a very long and winding path.

However first, we needed the all-important definition of a cryptid.

## Definition of a Crytid (*)

A cryptid is an animal that Cryptozoology seeks and believes to be alive and hidden in the present world. It is currently unclassified by Western science and meets the following criteria:

Must have a corporeal body, not spiritual or supernatural in nature

Must have no evidence of a previous existence in the fossil record or in existing recorded history (this would be an animal science had classified as extinct and then rediscovered)

Must not be totally mythological or legendary in origin, history, or recent history

Must not be based on only stories of spiritual beliefs of indigenous peoples

Must have verified documented witnesses

Must have verified documented evidence if recovered from sighting

Must be still considered unknown if animal was previously captured and lost with no verified documented evidence (i.e. Jacko)

Must not be based on a single article, sighting, or book

Must not be an interpretation of an individual's personal opinion

Documentation is of recorded names of witnesses, time, date, place, and exact information of sighting. No documentation may be anonymous nor evidence obtained from anonymous sources without a collaborating sworn testimony from a known source and supporting documentation as to why these sources must remain anonymous from the public record, i.e. age, employment, privacy

Examples of tangible evidence consist of hair, feathers, scales, feces/scat, body fluids, body remains, skeletal remains, and foot/paw/hand prints. (Note: Any uncontaminated evidence, other than prints, listed here can be tested, if viable DNA is present, for identification of donor animal.)

*Please keep in mind the relatively new science Cryptozoology and its cryptids are unique to this world. The definition of Cryptid cannot and is not all-inclusive or exclusive. Every unknown beast, strange sighting, and questionable report must be individually examined, considered, and retained for future possible documentation and evaluation.

### Cryptid Definition by Deborah Kaye Shira & Jerry D. Coleman

The first 'cryptid' by many to come to mind and to make some scream "foul" is the Coelacanth. However, it does not and could not fit into this outline. Nevertheless, one must understand the Coelacanth never was a cryptid and is, of course, not one now.

Simply put in this analogy, it is the meteoroid, meteor, meteorite name game: (1) millions of potential meteoroids fly around the cosmos, which may be bits of broken off asteroids, others, mere cosmic dust cast off by comets but not until it enters our atmosphere (2) is it a meteor, then the meteor becomes the meteorite (3) when on the ground.

A cryptid is an unknown living animal: (1) there may be numerous potential cryptids in the wild forests or deep under the seas yet to be considered. Once a creature is encountered in one form or another to be sought out (2) it then becomes a cryptid and "on the ground" e.g. discovered, a cryptid is not a cryptid, (3) it is a known animal accepted and classified by modern science.

Once the cryptid definition was determined, Deborah Shira rough drafted an outline on committee protocol and cryptid classification of categories. After a little, very little tweaking, the Categories I through VI emerged as something we could work with and was readily accepted by the members on the Cryptid Confirmation Committee.

## Committee Protocol

### RESEARCH:
1. A list of approximately 20-25 cryptids will be issued to the commitee on a weekly basis. The list will be posted on Monday.

2. Committee members will research all cryptids on the list utilizing acceptable sources of information. Acceptable forms of information are:
- Legitimate newspapers --- no sensationalist papers/tabloids should be considered
- Recognized Cryptozoology reference books
- University/college research libraries
- Legitimate websites
- Documentation of expeditions
- Legitimate magazine publications i.e. National Geographic, Smithsonian

3. Information obtained should be filled out following the basic form supplied and e-mailed to the collator for organizing. Information should be sent no later than Sunday. (A separate form should be filled out for each sighting of a cryptid. i.e. three sightings would require three seperate forms to be filled out. Do not put all three on one.)

4. If no information can be found on a cryptid, fill in the form with name of cryptid, your name, and No Information Found. Submit this form to the collator.

### DISCUSSION OF RESEARCH
1. The collated information will be posted on the forum for open discussion and debate the following Monday. (In cases of cryptids with a large amount of documentation, the week after)

2. Discussions and questions should occur in a serious, professional manner.
3. Any updates or changes to submit forms should be forwarded to the collator as soon as possible with UPDATED marked on the form.


## *DETERMINATION OF CRYPTID CLASSIFICATION*
1. Utilizing the information obtained and considerations from the discussion forum, committee members will vote by Sunday.
2. Committee members will determine by a 75% margin if a cryptid is a legitimate possibility (Category I & II) or inconsequential at this time (Category III, IV ,V& VI).
3. Cryptids can be updated at any time if new evidence is found. New evidence should be brought to the collator's immediate attention by filing a new research form, marked UPDATED, so the appropriate action can be taken.

*Category I* (Most verifiable with recent history and evidence to exist)
1.Multiple source documented cases of similar to identical examples of tangible evidence.
2. Multiple source documented sightings with descriptions, which are fundamentally equivalent.
3. Source documented photographic evidence.
4. Source documented audio evidence.
5. History of sightings within the last 100 years to present.
6. Has a recognizable territory/territories or pattern of travel with a history of sightings documented by the local population.

*Category II*
1. Multiple source documented sightings with descriptions, which are fundamentally equivalent.
2. Source documented photographic evidence.
3. Source documented audio evidence.
4. History of sightings within the last 200 years to present.
5. Has a recognizable territory/territories or pattern of travel with a history of sightings documented by the local population.

*Category III*
1. Multiple non-documented and/or unreliable sources of similar to identical sightings.
2. Photographic evidence of unknown origin.
3. Questionable physical evidence.
4. Audio of unknown origin.

*Category IV*
1. One sighting, non-documented and/or unreliable source(s).

*Category V*
1. Probable misidentification of known animal with no evidence.

*Category VI*
1. Hoax

Examples of tangible evidence consist of hair, feathers, scales, feces/scat, body fluids, body remains, skeletal remains, and foot/paw/hand prints. (Note: Any uncontaminated evidence, other than prints, listed here can be tested, if viable DNA is present, for identification of donor animal.)

Photographic evidence can be pictures, slides, or video, which have not been altered in any manner.

Any alterations to either photographs or audio and the evidence will be disallowed.

No pseudonym of either researcher or witness is allowed. If a pseudonym is used, it must be assigned a reason for its use and the real name placed in files not to be revealed to the public.

Documentation is of recorded names of witnesses, time, date, place, and exact information of sighting. No documentation may be anonymous nor evidence obtained from anonymous sources without a collaborating sworn testimony from a known source and supporting documentation as to why these sources must remain anonymous from the public record, i.e. age, employment, privacy, etc.

While Deborah Shira was tied up with the logistics, I was on a campaign quest to find qualified volunteers and setup the groups' website. Our volunteers first had to exhibit a true devotion to the task and an understanding of its importance. Other requirements were integrity, trust, commonsense, a thorough comprehension of Cryptozoology and a known history of productive dissension when warranted. The last thing the committee needed was a bunch of "yes men or women". Out of over 50 requests to join, 12 volunteers were accepted and passed the needed requirements with excellence.

A few problems with unknown "interested parties" e-mailing or telephoning me arose, claiming to be someone or something they were not, but these folks were easily detected and eliminated for consideration. The membership agenda also sought to gather representatives from different regions, not only from coast to coast in the United States, but worldwide. I believe we succeeded and on Saturday, June 12, 2004, we "turned on the lights and opened the doors" to the Cryptid Confirmation Committee!

# Statement from Deborah Shira,
## Cryptid Committee Chairperson:

When Jerry Coleman advanced the idea of forming a committee to investigate the plausibility of a list of "cryptids" and to set the groundwork for establishing Cryptozoology on firmer ground as a science, I immediately volunteered my services. I anticipated a chance to make a difference in the biased and insular minds of those who denounce Cryptozoology as "fringe science" or as that which is radical and unconventional.

When all methods and procedures were established, Jerry brought onboard a remarkable group of people. These individuals have utilized their personal time, at no compensation, to further a mutual aspiration for the future of Cryptozoology. This excellent group of people are as follows: Gerry Bacon of Michigan, Cathy Clark of California, Robert Coppen, author and artist of New York, Ivan Garrett, Jr. B.S. in Zoology/Physiology of Wyoming, Keith Olsen, Paul Rheaume of New Hampshire, Aimee Weis, Daniel Falconer, Conceptual Designer and Writer for Film and Television of New Zealand, Zach Fang of Maryland and others.

*Please note there are other members I would like to acknowledge but for personal reasons did not wish their names to be published at this time.

We started with a list of seven hundred and eighty four (784) cryptids. As the research progressed we recognized we had a serious dilemma on our hands. We would discover that the list was a convoluted collection of myths, legends, supernatural entities, known animals, multiple names, and misidentifications, many of which were interwoven. The list grows on a weekly basis as, during our research, we uncover other cryptids not on the original list. Some of the complexities of the list have inured in us the need to look in depth at each and every listing, to analyze and dissect each and every detail to discover the truth. Some have given us cause for mirth as the plausibility is so ludicrous to even be considered, but consider it we must as to remain open minded and impartial.

To date (30 August 2005), of the original list of 784 cryptids, we have achieved the following results:

```
ELIMINATED DUE TO NO INFORMATION FOUND............ 218
ELIMINATED DUE TO CRYPTID IS KNOWN ANIMAL .........150
ELIMINATED DUE TO MYTH/LEGEND............................101
ELIMINATED DUE TO SUPERNATURAL ENTITY..................14
ELIMINATED DUE TO LOCAL NAME FOR LISTED CRYPTID...54
```

CRYPTID CATEGORY I.....................1
  Discovered: Bili/Bondi ape

CRYPTID CATEGORY II.........12
  1. Mangden - hoofed deer, Vietnam
  2. Quang Khem - deer, Vietnam
  3. Malagnira - lemur, Madagascar
  4. Tzuchinoko - snake, Japan
  5. Bigfoot/Sasquatch - hominid, United States
  6. Almas - hominid, Asia
  7. Nguoi-Rung - hominid, China
  8. Nittaewo - hominid, Sri Lanka
  9. Orang Gadang - hominid, Indonesia
  10. Orang Pendek - hominid, Indonesia
  11. Ye-Ren - hominid, China
  12. Yeti - hominid, Himalayas

CRYPTID CATEGORY III......................27
  Top dozen of Category III:

1. Mongolian goat-antelope - Mongolia
2. Shunka Warak'in - wolf, United States
3. Waitoreke - otter, New Zealand
4. Pe De Garrafa - primate, brazil
5. Ren-Xiong - primate, China
6. Sisemite - primate, Central America
7. Kongamato - flying reptile, Zambia
8. Lummis's Pichu-cuate - snake, United States
9. Olitiau - flying reptile, Cameroon
10. Makalala - bird, East Africa
11. Trinity Alps Giant Salamander - salamander, United States
12. Mapinguari - giant ground sloth, South America

CRYPTID CATEGORY IV...........................41
CRYPTID CATEGORY V...........................61

TOTAL CRYPTIDS ELIMINATED......................................542
TOTAL CRYPTIDS MEETING REQUIREMENTS.........142
TOTAL RESEARCHED to Date....................................684

For well over a year, our committee has been researching the plausibility of a list of cryptids. It has been a very enlightening work, providing insight into the minds of the human species as well as the possibility of the unknown existing. Our reactions have ranged from laughter at the ludicrous, awe at the possibility, puzzlement at the conclusions drawn from non-existent evidence, anger at purposeful hoaxing and distortion of facts and evidence, and exaltation at the discovery of one of our Category I cryptids. (More on this topic will be provided later.)

Throughout the research, certain divisions begin to emerge in the reporting of cryptids. These divisions are the result of experience, knowledge, racial background, religious background and a variety of other influences faced by the human species on a day to day basis, some influenced by the very quest for survival. Let us look at these influences separately and how they affect the report of a cryptid sighting.

Let us begin with the more plausible of the cryptids. Case in point is our Category I cryptid, which is no longer a cryptid but a known animal, the Bili/Bondi ape. The hunters of the indigenous peoples reported the existence of an ape that looked like a chimpanzee but acted like a gorilla. It was reputed to be extremely aggressive and was nicknamed the "lion killer" because of its propensity for violence and ability to kill an adult male lion. Rumors of this animal reached the outside world and research proved the existence of the animal. It is now being scientifically analyzed to determine if the Bili/Bondi ape is a new species/sub-species or if is a case of evolution occurring in front of us with an isolated group of chimps adapting to new conditions. Facts were stated, research done and the case was solved.

Not all cryptids are solved with the ease of the Bili/Bondi ape. Indigenous peoples, regardless of conversion to "enlightened religions," still retain the beliefs and superstitions of the past and incorporate them into their present beliefs. Therefore, demons, spirits, and supernatural animals are still an element of their present beliefs and as real as the family dog or other domestic animal. The result is that such ludicrous reports are received as that of the Mamlambo.

The Mamlambo is supposedly a 60 plus foot behemoth that inhabits African rivers of the Congo and neighboring countries. It has a head reminiscent of a horse, the body of a crocodile, and short, stubby legs. It is said to glow with a greenish color at night. It has a preference for human brains, which it attains by grabbing a non-suspecting victim from the shore, dragging them into the river, where upon it holds the victim under until drowned. The Mamlambo then rips off the face and sucks out the brain. Why a 60 foot plus creature would show a predilection for brains is somewhat fuzzy, when with it's size, in my opinion, it would be more prone to treat a human as a chicken nugget and indulge in the treat by popping the victim into it's mouth whole. It would take a lot of brains to fill up an animal of that size, devastating whole villages, which, one would think be newsworthy and we would be apt to open our papers and read of villages disappearing every day. Here the modus operandi of the animal in question, grabbing victims from the bank, drowning them, then indulging in it's meal is exactly that of a large crocodile. The crocodile is endemic to the area. Another example is the Nandi bear, which has habits paralleling those of a large hyena. Again, another animal populating the area where the Nandi bear is said to roam.

Is the work we are engaged in important to the future of Cryptozoology? My personal opinion is "yes". As you can discern from the above statistics, the very things which have kept Cryptozoology a fringe science are being eliminated, leaving a realistic base of cryptids with the potential to be bona fide animals. We have observed how a common animal can evolve in the uneducated mind into a creature of mythic proportions. The hyena is a case in point. Their species characteristics and hunting habits are such that they can be ascribed as the source of many of the African cryptids. Feral dogs and cats the world over also transform into creatures of incredible proportions due to inaccuracies in reporting, exaggerations, and the want of media attention. Even the mundane and inanimate become creatures of cryptid status, such as the case of logs and waves becoming lake monsters.

Also the list, once cleared of the non-cryptids, must be maintained. Sightings and new information will continually be received which may result in a cryptid being moved to another category, being removed because it is identified as a known animal, or a cryptid is discovered and is awarded the distinction of being assigned as a new genus and/or species, making it a scientifically classified known animal. The continuation of the research being done is vital in the establishment of Cryptozoology as a science. The mythic and supernatural incursions must be eradicated and further infiltration of creatures of a nonscientific nature eliminated.

*D.K. Shira*

# 9. ADVANCED FIELD RESEARCH

As you get further into developing your own style of research, it will become mandatory that you find organized methods of acquiring and securing your findings. In short, extraordinary claims call for extraordinary proof. The devoted researcher will not have the luxury of the trial and error method. Experimenting along the way will only decrease your ability to accomplish the task or confirmation needed. Although, successfully investigating the unknown is no different from any other field investigation, where basic, yet solid information-gathering techniques are necessary.

However, unique to the Cryptozoology field is what you do with the information, as in who to notify and when to share it. One erroneous statement told as truth, or one assumption disguised as fact, will cost you your credibility. Without professional integrity little hope exists for your research to ever become more than entertainment or worse, a constant need to do damage control. As they say, 'Rome was not built in a day', nor will your investigation be. So triple check your data and seek out every available witness. Use logic, patience and vigilance as your partners. Every stone needs turned and must be looked at from all sides and confirmed as case fact. Before you reveal your investigation, play the role of the hardcore debunking skeptic. Ask yourself what they will ask, look at your evidence through their eyes and when you are satisfied -- do it all over again!

For me, I have chosen to run my own investigations of the unexplained like a small business. First, meet and greet your clients (your witnesses). Second, find trusted and reliable vendors (your information sources). Third, enlist sincere, devoted partners (your colleagues). Finally, and most importantly, give the customer a product you are proud of and can guarantee to be an example of honest and sincere work (your investigation to the public).

Words like "evidence" and "proof" incorrectly take on different meanings in this field. Do not fall into these traps. Evidence is good information for which a conclusion can be based, nothing less qualifies. Proof is convincing evidence and verification of the event, period. Speculations, theories, assumptions and opinions run rampant with skeptics and believers alike. Make sure you call it what it is. A sighting is not proof, it is testimony only and a track in the mud is not verification, but possible evidence at best. In short, mind your vocabulary, say what you mean and mean what you say. Do not confuse the issue for the sake of egotistical reasons or wishful thinking. Stick to the facts, document your findings and present your case when you are sure you have a case to present.

## Using a Questionnaire

A simple, yet good, start to any field investigation would be to have the witness or witnesses fill out a questionnaire. Do not let this stand in the way or replace a one-on-one personal interview though. Nothing beats watching the faces, noting the voice tone and observing the body movements of a real live witness. Ask any police officer about this. Your questionnaire should compliment the interview and document the event.

I have developed a 25-question form, which works for my needs and other researchers have utilized it with positive results. What follows is the complete field form used:

## Sighting Or Event Questionnaire

Please answer as many of the following questions as you can or wish to. Thank you for your cooperation.

### Personal Info:

1. Full name  _____
2. Age at time of event _____
3. Present address _____
If different from time of event, please add other


4. Sex _____
5. Education _____
6. Occupation _____
7. Religion _____
8. Telephone number _____
9. E-mail address _____
10. Height and weight; _____ _____

### Event Info:

11. What did you experience? _____
12. Where? Exact location and surroundings _____
13. When? Complete date and time _____
14. Any other witnesses? If so please list _____
15. Weather conditions; including temperature _____
16. Were you wearing eyeglasses or contacts at the time?
Do you need them? _____
17. Have you ever seen anything like this before? If yes please explain;
_____

18. How long did the sighting or event last? _____
19. What were you doing prior to the event? _____
20. What was the first thing you did after the event?
_____

**Description Info:**

21. In detail describe what happened _____
22. Completely explain what you did during the encounter?
_____
23. Describe or sketch the sighting the best you can?
_____
24. Note noises or unusual items you saw before, during or after the event: _____
25. List any comment you wish here, even theories:
_____

There are a few follow-up questions that are much more personal and should be asked only after the witness accepts the interview and seems open and willing to assist in the investigation. When you and the witness are both comfortable, follow up with detailed personal beliefs concerning legends and folklore. Inquire as to any open wounds or bleeding the witness may have had at the time of the encounter. Find out if any substance use, such as medication or alcohol, took place. Tactfully ask if they have any disorders or physical problems of any kind, even ones they may consider minor, such as color blindness, headaches, neck or back pains, near or far sightedness and even note the last time the witness claims to have had a good night's sleep.

The height / weight question (#10) I find important for a number of reasons. I am certainly not trying to trick anyone but there are a number of reasons why this information may become relevant. More times than not the answer, among other answers on the questionnaire, eliminates the eyewitness as a possible culprit in the encounter or strengthens their testimony when addressing the ever-present debunkers.

Reasons I ask such seemingly personal questions rarely asked by other researchers are:

1. In the Lawndale Big Bird, others have now put out the claim Marlon was 'over' 70 pounds and pass this on to the bird experts as actual documentation. We know, because I asked Marlon and his mother two days after the event, that the boy actually weighed close to 56 pounds. Yes, it is still an improbable weight for a bird to pick up but very different from 70-plus pounds. This arbitrary adding of 14 pounds dramatically changes the size of the bird due needed to lift him.

2. In another case, doubt was placed in a police officer's mind that the witness saw a 'Black Panther' running across his lawn from the far side of his vehicle ---- until I took out my notes. I told the officer the man [witness]

was 6 foot 3 inches and could easily see over the vehicle in question and at the angle he claimed. This changed things completely. Often times, I do re-enactments and re-create the sight line of the witness. A few inches here or there may change what can be seen from certain angles and conditions.

3. When it comes to tracks, the depth and stride can quickly eliminate lets say, our female eyewitness as a hoaxer. In this example, we will say that she is 5 foot 3 inches and weighs 105 pounds. The depth of a track can also be important in a case where a witness, or group of witnesses, claims to have seen something that was 7 foot tall and must have weighed 550 pounds.

4. The weight documents the possible physical ability of the witness. In one example, we can find it more likely that a witness that was 145 pounds and 6 feet tall ran around a barn in pursuit, or in terror, of a thing that he saw than a man who was elderly and weighed 275 pounds.

Most of this is obvious and is included merely to be thorough but most importantly, it is on record. Once the form is filled out and your field notes are compared to it, you should have a fairly comprehensive history of the event and witness.

## The Eyewitness

The first step in a thorough interview is to fully introduce yourself. Speak about a few minor, but personal, topics in your life and show the person you are open, honest and sincere. This will relax your witness and create a sense of trust. Then direct your attention to them but do not talk about the encounter yet. Compliment their house, garden, vehicle or even their shirt. People usually love to talk about themselves or their family. Casually ask about their children, mate or place of employment.

Slowly and carefully, begin the examination of the sighting. Do not lead the witness or assume anything. Always ask their permission before photographing or taping anything. Let them lead you to the site or next topic and only ask for clarification at this point, not personal theories.

When the event testimony is documented, take the next step and find out about any physical problems your witness may have, as already stated. Then look around the area slowly and carefully, look for any additional witnesses and ask your witness of that possibility. The possible additional witnesses could be many, from a neighbor to a construction worker, a repairman in the area, mail carrier, pizza delivery person or even a police officer called to the scene.

Tactfully ask your witness about their personal beliefs and theories. Make it known that nothing shocks you and that all angles must be considered. This will give your witness a true sense of relief that you are willing to openly listen to them and not judge them.

You will soon find out that, for many eyewitnesses, ths investigative work is not very important to them. Their story may be told to you at a dinner party or while waiting in a doctor's office but for them to actually take their time to pick up the telephone or travel to a meeting place to discuss their case seems like an inconvenience and does not happen very often. Eyewitnesses will tell their experiences, even grant interviews, but then sometimes will seem to fall off the face of the earth after the telling of it. Scores of times, I have waited for a telephone call or letter that was promised but never came or have experienced an interview that was cut short due to an unrelated reason.

Is the eyewitness testimony more of a question of accuracy than honesty? More of logic than assumption? May another answer be derived from the sensationalized reporting of events rather than the events themselves? Alternatively, is it prudent and harmless to stop for a moment, listen to the testimony, examine an area, photograph a site then logically, honestly and diplomatically tally up the findings, evaluate the case and document it accordingly?

Of course, there are thousands of misidentifications, hundreds of hoaxes, pranks and jokes, scores of released and escaped animals and numerous legendary shadowy sightings. However, what about the others, what about the one in a hundred or even the one in a million sighting? Can we afford to close our eyes or debunk it all? I think not. I think the oceans run too deep and the forests remain too dark. Recent history alone is the yardstick of proof. Animals exist that we have yet to discover and this is something that I am 100% sure of.

Witnesses are regular people with routines and other plans; plans that do not include cryptids or ghost stories in their day to day life. Skeptics may conclude an unwilling witness is an untruthful witness. Believers would conclude the unwilling witness is a scared or confused witness. Generally speaking though, an unwilling eyewitness is simply a person that experienced something unique and realizes little or no understanding of it will ever be gained and goes on about their business.

Being aware of this lack of witness interest, then makes it imperative for you to gather as much information, testimony, photographs and sketches as you possibly can obtain during what may be not only your first but last interview with the eyewitness. Even if you have a very willing and interested witness, unforeseen events may follow that would make further interviews impossible. Some reasons might include death, religious changes, occupational concerns, moving without a forwarding address, another researchers story written up that would upset the witness or even threats from unknown sources (some claim men-in-black or pranksters). So get the information while you can and consider any follow-up interviews that you might get to do as an added bonus.

## Follow-up Interviews

One tool that I have added to my investigative arsenal in recent years has been a toll free number. Once contact has been made with a new witness, the number is given to them and they are instructed to call anytime they desire to add to or update the encounter. This trust and interest I have shown has paid off with huge dividends. Many people would rather talk directly to the investigator, at their convenience, thus knowing they are being heard and understood when they are in the mood to talk. Another plus is my ability to further question them, on the spot, exposing or exploring other testimony.

In addition to telephone calls, e-mails, snail mail, faxes and word of mouth are all in the mix. I personally receive an average of three new reports each week about phantom panther sightings and this is without any personal campaigning for the chronicles. Once received, all encounters, no matter how bizarre on the surface, are taken seriously and recorded. The most promising, that is the most detailed report, with supporting information enclosed in which to contact the eyewitnesses, receive immediate attention.

One of the most interesting cases I have been associated with is the Lawndale Big Bird attempted abduction of young Marlon Lowe. Literal hundreds of hours, numerous interviews and follow-ups have revolved around this case. There have been many follow-up investigations and each of them has added more confirmation of the original event. I stated it earlier but it's worth repeating --- you case will always be under construction.

# Evidence Gathering

### Roadkill

Scores of cryptid sightings are in conjunction with roadkills, either because the creature was going after the roadkill or was struck by a vehicle and became one itself. Witnesses often claim to see a dashing glimpse of an unknown beast as it snatches up a dead opossum from the roadway or they pass a large hairy beast, so obliterated by numerous 18-wheelers that the once magnificent unknown animal is reduced to nothing more than a throw rug. Never are any of these claims of a squashed Sasquatch sampled for DNA ---- but let me rephrase that ---- almost never is a sample collected but when the claim of a sample is collected, the evidence mysteriously vanishes on its way to or while in the lab.

First, of course, is the needed skill to identify roadkill yourself. Question what was seen, stop and exam it and if deemed unknown, collect a sample and snap a few photographs. If the roadkill has been feasted upon, examination of it is imperative. Please do not try this activity alone. Have an associate watch the traffic, pull well off the road, only in good weather and daylight hours, and never stop where it is illegal to park. The last thing we need is for you to become roadkill yourself! If you do see a roadkill in a dangerous, location call the county and ask them to record what the kill was. I have found they will be glad to do this for you.

After speaking with three different animal control officers in three different States (IL, KY, & TN), they repeated the following four areas as high kill zones. The places to be on high alert for roadkills are by bridges, construction areas, long, straight rural roadways and thick, wooded lanes.

Bridge areas yield a high number of road kills for obvious reasons --- water is a natural need and an attraction to predators waiting for a meal, secondly the animal becomes contained on or by a bridge with nowhere to flee from oncoming traffic.

Construction areas have a history of high volume road kills as well, ask any road worker. Here, the animals seem to become disoriented due to the new landscaping and noise in the construction zone. They also tend to cross the roadway more often as the construction often forces them from their homes and sends them looking for a new location.

Long straight roadways also yield a fair amount of roadkills. Animal control agents surmise it must be due to automobile speeds increasing and animals, unaware of the danger, simply stroll into the path.

Lastly, thick wooded lanes also produce their fair share of kills. These lanes normally seem to catch the critters completely by surprise as they blindly walk into the path of a vehicle. Here, the roadkill may never be noticed due to being thrown into a weedy ditch or quickly eaten by other wildlife.

Be vigilant in your search and examination of road kill. What looks like a large black dog may be our elusive black panther. If in doubt, snap a couple of photographs, grab a hair specimen and record the exact location, time and conditions.

### Tracking

Since your quarry is largely "unknown", little documentation exists about it, so we have to adapt what we know from the known species and apply those same tracking techniques. Of course, what you are most likely to run across while tracking a cryptid will be signs from known species. Study your target area's animals, people and terrain. Knowing and eliminating these identifiable markings will have you one up on the novice and well on your way to having true outdoor experience and in-the-field credibility.

Tracking is much more involved than luckily stumbling on that one muddy paw print. What to look for listen for and even smell in the woods will be covered in Chapter 10, so for now, let us seek out actual tracking techniques and know where and what to look for.

First, brush up on all the exact identifications of the paw and hoof tracks of the area and bring a field guide with you for conformation. General knowledge of family species classifications is very useful. For instance, a canine track is oval and one could draw an imaginary X from heel pad to outer toes. A feline track usually has no claw marks and is usually wider than longer.

The term "tracking signs", which are anything other than tracks themselves, are of the utmost importance to recognize. These signs may equate to 75 percent of your tracking. First on one's agenda should be reading the landscape to locate animals. Animals exist in what are called "animal islands". Once you have located an herbivore island, the carnivores are not far behind. To find an herbivore island look for cover, downed trees, tangled brush, rocks to hide in and escape to. Then, study the vegetation, look for various types of plants in a single area that will supply food all year around. Keep in mind that for the herbivore to venture too far out of its island may mean death. Do not assume the island needs a supply of water. Herbivores can get enough from the plants, dew and rain puddles. Seeing one of these animals, such as the squirrel, rabbit or deer would indicate an area might need a second look. Seeing two of them would bring the status to "good" and seeing all three would bring the value to "excellent". Your best field location would be in a "transitional zone", such as field to forest, woods to stream or creek to field. This is where you will find the largest variety of growth and cover.

Next, look for "passages". Animals, like humans, take the easiest, fastest route. Look for "trails", the forest's highway system. Trampled down dead grasses and unnatural gaps in bushes are signs. Then, seek out animal "runs", mud slides by the waterway, paths connecting bedding or feeding areas that may also lead back to the trails. Signs vary from matted down grass, where a deer was just sleeping, to smooth mud along the bank of a creek that a muskrat frequents. Ripe berries completely stripped from only one bush reveals birds were not the culprits but a bear and torn bark from a tree does not mean a large cat must have done it but more likely a white-tail buck.

The "signs" in the forest to help track the animal are numerous including broken twigs, stone roles, bedding areas, scratches in the dirt and trees, chew marks on grass, hair and feathers, scat droppings and rubs or polished areas. These all are 'signs' not to be ignored.

**Remember these four basic tracking steps:**
1. Learn your track identification at a glance.
2. Bring a field guide to confirm the identity.
3. Learn how to look for "animal islands".
4. Take note of all "tracking signs".

## Casting

In past years, plaster of paris was used for casting animal tracks. However, it is now recommended that only dental stone be used. Dental stone results in a superior cast, is more durable and harder and can be cleaned with a potassium sulfate solution with very little loss or erosion of detail. These days of examining or seeking the dermal ridges of a cast is foremost on the minds of interested parties. Dental stone is available from any local dental supply store. Experiment by making a few test casts of your feet or your pets before ruining potential evidence.

For complete and detailed techniques on making a cast and mixing procedures, please refer to Dwayne S. Hilderbrand, CLPE, Lead Latent Print Examiner, Scottsdale Police Crime Lab, author of the book "Footwear, The Missed Evidence" or go to www.crime-scene-investigator.net .

## The Value of Re-creations

The tool of re-creating a scene or event is one that I often use in one form or another. Whether it is an unknown beast or paranormal event, a re-creation can at times reveal answers or understanding that one cannot get while sitting in front of their computer.

If a re-creation is attempted, match as many of the details in the testimony as can be done. This includes time of day, temperature and season, height of the witness, position of the witness or witnesses, clothes worn, exact location or area, means of travel and speed, etc.

Some readers may be familiar with the numerous re-creations and field testing I have done in the past. These re-creations may reveal a hoax or in some cases, even further document an unknown encounter.

Re-creations are far from scientific, yet are much more valuable in forming a theory than simple assumptions or guesswork, which is too often found to be utilized by a "tool-less, clueless" researcher.

### Cryptid Scene Investigation

The initials for this are likely to spur recognition in the minds of many readers and in this case, you can also think of this as a "crime scene investigation" or CSI. Investigating cryptids may be even tougher than investigating crimes though because every one of your "scenes" is already contaminated. The scene may be days, if not weeks or even months, old and without a laboratory or unlimited funds at your disposal, adding no authority to insist anyone cooperate, all the cards are stacked against you from the start.

Photographs and sketches are yet another piece of the evidence that must be acquired. These photos and sketches may later be dismissed by some as hoaxes or imagination at work but that is not your concern at this time. You concern is to gather what you can and present it --- nothing more and nothing less. Label everything collected, take plaster casts when possible, photograph every angle and look for the obvious or out of place. In short, do not overlook or assume anything.

Again, I must add, seek out and attend seminars of related, useful topics. A seminar on greeting and meeting people will be more helpful in the field than attending a Star Trek convention. An Anthropology conference will add more to your ability than a Hollywood-hyped Sasquatch movie. Never stop learning and developing your skills.

Record, record, record ---- measure distances, structure heights, landscaping layouts, area noises, smells, and soil types. Look around! look through the eyes of the witness and creature. See what they saw, smell what they smelled, hear what they heard. Is there a neighbor peeking out of the window at you? You may have found another potential witness! Does the air have the smell of an old forest fire that may have been responsible for the beast's unexpected exposure? Is the wind whistling through a loose roof tile? This may explain our witness' claim that the animal made high-pitched sounds.

This may be your one and only opportunity to totally investigate the area and it certainly will be your best time.

### Expeditions

When you are ready --- and you will know it ---- the next natural step to take for genuine seekers of the unexplained is an expedition. Often repeated misconceptions of an expedition are that it takes place in a far away land, must be sponsored, spans over a few months and must have a team of highly educated individuals accompanying the expedition. All of this is false!

Another often-repeated mistake I hear over and over again is that the field researcher makes expedition plans for --- and only for ---- large creatures like the African cryptid Mokele-Mbembe, a believed living dinosaur, or Nessie at Lock Ness. Such expeditions are not only extremely expensive and well out of the price range for the average researcher but are very time consuming and require vast experience in dozens of fields that most do not have. It is wonderful to have big dreams but don't dream so big that you wake up one day 20 years later and realize that you have never gone anywhere!

The wise and efficient individual looks in his "own backyard" first! Organize the event to fit your schedule and pocketbook. Gather trusted and interested friends or associates. Bring equipment you already own, can borrow or fit your budget. The advantages in searching your own region go beyond the financial savings you will experience. Who better knows the area than you do? Who can better talk to the locals in a completely understanding way, thus opening doors (land access), where strangers may find it off limits? Adding your knowledge of local laws, local folklore and local history will all be a plus. Then, rest assured you will come back with "something" - --- and that "something" will be experience.

Learn as much about the area of your expedition as you can. Know exactly where your camp will be and where you can replenish your supplies. Bring maps of the area, obtain knowledge of the local wildlife and the local people, study the past legends, past expeditions and last but far from least, know where the closest medical facility is located.

In the search for these cryptids, studying their food supply may lead to answers. If we seek these animals without a game plan it is easy for a cryptid to avoid us while we are in its territory. But while the beast is consumed in thought with hunger and on the path for dinner, this may be the edge needed to tip the scale to the investigator's advantage. Know where the berry patches are and the fresh water springs. Know the local wildlife and its habits and be alert for activity at all times, especially in the evening, night and dawn hours.

When the preparation is done, and you've arrived on location, notify the local law enforcement, rangers or landowner of your presences. Then, check and secure supplies and set-up camp, familiarize yourself with the surroundings (look, listen and smell), eat a good meal and get some rest. Don't head out in search of mystery creatures while too excited or too tired. This is a scientific expedition, so treat it as such by being at your top form and totally prepared.

### Your Best Asset

No matter what tools or high-tech gadgets you might have to help in your search for answers to the mysterious questions of cryptids, the best asset that you can have is yourself. Don't rely on the computer, newspapers, magazines or television shows to steer you to the next event. Hit the fields of the unexplained, seek out witnesses, and scour the countryside in search of the unknown. Many people will never come forward or report a strange sighting to anyone outside of a trusted few. You should take a personal interest and only then will someone's friend, neighbor, or even a family member reveal that they have a  story to tell.

Some people simply don't know how to explain a unique encounter and will make excuses for their testimony from the get go. Trust is the key in this and in almost every other situation. Let them know right up front that you are serious, have heard this before and do not judge or assume anything.

If you believe in yourself, others will believe in you too.

# 10. THE SILENT WOODS AROUND US
## With Gerry Bacon

**W**ould we dare go into an unfamiliar forest, patiently waiting for hours, listening, watching and seeking out those unknown noises and eerie shadows as they glide by, only then to ask what lurks within those woods? Evidently, many of us contemplate it and do so. Thousands hike, camp, hunt, fish and at times, casually stroll through the woods and forests simply to find tranquility away from a confused and busy world. Sighting a migrating bird or unique track eases the soul and plants our feet back firmly on the ground with the knowledge that another world, apart from the city lights and busy streets, co-exists in a primitive and peaceful form around us.

Crypto-hunting has become a favorite past time for many new believers and old skeptics. Cryptozoology has evolved from book reading to a new plateau in this new millennium. It is now an activity, a hunt, an investigation. Numerous reasons may be attributed to this mini-phenomenon of self-expansion into exploration and adventure ---- a quest for new life, a thirst for explanation or an excitement only found by discovering nature.

It is somewhat of a risk to venture into our timber, even those state parks that pepper the countryside. Every wooded region has its fair share of unexplained sighting and danger. Unknown and unconfirmed reports of large black panthers, mysteriously crop up from time to time in any area. Hairy bipedal creatures have been reported, more as real than legend, throughout the United States, as well as numerous other countries. The Chupacabra continues to be reported raiding farms of the Southern United States and Central America. Large boa constrictors are pulled from the swamps of Florida, not to mention, thought to be extinct or undiscovered birds continue are being reported. Even dinosaurs have been recently allegedly seen in South America and yes, lake and sea beasts still produce a fuzzy photo from time to time. The stories are out there, the undocumented tales and misidentifications pull us to an adventure where maybe --- just maybe ---- it will be one of us who reveals the fraud or discovers the creature for what it truly is.

However, before you dive head first into the silent woods around us, be aware of the risk ---- a risk too often not seen or one you walk right into. These dangers are more numerous than all the cryptids put together, more relentless than a stalking cougar and rest assured much more likely to strike than a charging pack of wolves. They often come from below as you are looking forward or from above as you are looking down. Too often you may not even see them until the pain makes itself known. These foes turn you into the prey in some cases and come as mosquitos carrying diseases like Encephalitis (St. Louis, Western Equine, La Crosse, Eastern Equine, and West Nile), Dengue Fever, Malaria and Yellow Fever, and as ticks carrying Rocky Mountain spotted fever and Lyme disease. Then there are biting flies, annoying gnats, killer bees, wasps, fleas, venomous snakes under logs and venomous spiders, like the Brown Recluse or Black Widow, that you may walk right into. Don't forget the leeches and snapping turtles, waiting in the creek. Even scorpions that most believe live only in the desert yet have many habitats, which also include forests, grasslands and caves.

However, it does not stop there. Challenge yourself to recognize poisonous plants. Poison ivy, poison oak and poison sumac should be identifiable to you at a glance. These plants, and the mentioned little varmints, can ruin an outing and in some cases, put you at serious risk in a hurry! Keep a first aid kit with you at all times and know how to use it!

An even more deadly danger to be heeded when searching the silent woods from from man rather than the elusive creatures you hunt. Man finds these woods the perfect place to hide meth amphetamine labs or marijuana crops. Even hidden moonshine stills in some of the southern states are becoming a problem once again due to tax hikes, acquiring licenses and the ever-present looming dark clouds of lawsuits. Illegal alcohol avoids these obstacles. Then, you have people on the run from the law hiding and traveling through the woods and even at times, one can come upon a homeless person or runaway teen. Gun-toting poachers and kids ready to shoot anything that moves lurk around many bushes. You should also beware of traps set for fur-bearing animals. Sometimes these traps are abandoned but still set and just as dangerous. I have seen all of these things in the woods over the years. Venturing into our woods and forests requires a heighten awareness for the human species --- up to no good, dangerous and irresponsible --- rather than the unknown creature lurking in the shadows.

Now that I have cautioned the reader of everything breathing, creeping and crawling in the forest, I warn you to be alert to the challenges of the landscaping and weather. The beauty of the landscape can be just as dangerous as all of these other things, from falling rocks and mudslides to swift undercurrents and slippery mosses. The possibility of unpredictable weather should be kept in mind during that gorgeous mid-morning hike. Nature's pruning (heavy winds) can bring a tree or large limb down on you faster than you can say, "Cryptozoologist!" A flash flood could block your path or trap you if no plan to escape from the dry creek bed was made in advance. Moreover, even that gorgeous day holds its demon's with sun rash, heat exhaustion, heat stoke and heat cramps.

These safe and silent woods around us are anything but silent if you know how to listen and far from safe, unless you know how to read the signs and identify potential danger.

Now, allow me to introduce you to the insight and wisdom of a long time outdoorsman, Mr. Gerry Bacon of Detroit, Michigan. Bacon, now 50 years young and proud father of five great children still makes a comfortable living driving a truck. His interest in Cryptozoology reaches back to the mid-1960's and another equal interest, and perhaps even longer love, has been his hundreds of hunting and fishing excursions over the years.

I would call Gerry Bacon an expert witness when it comes to anything to do with the outdoors. He is a man that balances his knowledge of cryptid description with an honest open skepticism. He has personal hands-on field and forest experiences, which compliments literally hundreds of thousands of road miles. It is from the miles he has logged and locations he has seen that places Bacon in the unique position of being a man to listen to when examining glimpses of creatures, fleeting shadows atop a tree line or woodland noises unlike any usually heard.

His interests and life mix well between driving a truck, being an active outdoorsman and having a fascination with cryptids. Bacon had seen and identified thousands of roadkills over the years and realizes how easy it would be to misidentify an animal after being struck at 70 miles an hour by an 18-wheeler. He has also witnessed thousands of other animals running, moving and hiding under every imaginable condition, whether it be good or inclement weather, poor and bright lighting or even partial glimpses at a distance.

Another facet of his trucking job worth acknowledging is Bacon's tendency to end up in many of the industrial parks that border our cities and suburbs, often extending to the open countryside. This synthetic buffer, which the industrial park provides, has created an area where man meets animal. It's a zone that places the animals on the edge of a populated area, but not too close to the city, and its a place that is not busy or populated after dark. Bacon has found himself in one of these parks on many nights, waiting for an 8:00 a.m. dock appointment, having arrived hours too early. These are long, lonely nights for many people, sleep would be difficult and the dark expanses of woods and open ground might give rise to dreams born of the imagination. This is not the case with Gerry Bacon though...

***What follows are Gerry Bacon's personal observations and advice in his own words:***

I was pushing through a thicket of Tag alder, bent over double when I spotted it ---- a large pile of scat lying in the middle of the deer trail I was following. I was not sure what it was, but was positive what it was not. It was not deer or rabbit, nor dog-like, so I doubted coyote. As I studied it, I suddenly felt very uneasy. I heard nothing unusual, smelled nothing offensive, but still, the feeling persisted. I looked around and saw nothing to account for my feeling. To this day, I don't know why I felt I should leave, but leave I did. I backed out of the tangle and continued my explorations elsewhere.

I have hunted this particular area for over thirty years and have never felt uncomfortable here before or since. In fact, that fall I took a stand not a hundred yards from this very spot, a slight ridge separating two swamps. Why the uneasiness this time? The answer could be of the reported black bear (Ursus americanus), that had been seen in the area that particular summer.

When I first started hunting the area of Gladwin County, Michigan back in 1968, there were no bears, at least no resident bears. Although, recalling as a child my aunt and I would walk down a sandy trail near my grandparent's cabin, oftentimes finding unmistakable bear tracks. In 1973, I shot a small buck on the west side of Three River Road, almost directly across from the recent incident. Several days later, a black bear was killed after threatening to charge a hunter less than a

half a mile from where I had taken my deer. So, while there have always been transitory bears moving through this region, it's only been the past few years that it can be claimed that bears are native to this region.

I had never seen bear scat before. I have since identified it through pictures but at the time, I really had nothing more than an idea of what it may look like. The bear that left it was not in the immediate vicinity as far as I know. Certainly, there was nothing there to lead me to believe it was still around. I heard nothing out of the ordinary. I smelled no foul odors, which are normally associated with bears. So why was I so uneasy? Why did I feel that the prudent thing for me to do was to immediately retreat? Not just, walk on, but also to return the way I came. Was I in danger? I don't believe I was.

As I look back on the episode with the relief that time and distance provide. I honestly believe I had no more to fear that bright, sunny August day than I have on those cold, predawn November mornings, snaking my way along an oak ridge or picking my way through a cedar swamp. I cannot explain why I felt that discretion demanded I leave that day. But I've come to trust my senses when in the woods and never been in any real danger. Been turned around for several hours at times but always found my way out. I've gotten so cold that I have built a fire with my hands on a cold, rainy day. I've broken through ice and been soaked to the waist in weather so cold the rabbits wouldn't come out of their dens and even once had to wait for my bootlaces to thaw out so that I could untie them when I got back to the cabin. I've been scratched by branches, stabbed by thorns, tripped by rocks and almost always wind up with something in my eye, but I've never been in any real danger. Yet that one time, I was afraid.

If I, an experienced outdoorsman, can be so rattled by an innocuous pile of scat lying in a trail, what of the person who ventures into the wilds only occasionally, especially someone searching for monstrous beasts or living legends? What must that person think who hears a Great Horned Owl hooting at dusk, when the only owls he has ever heard were from a horror movie? What of the young lady, driving a lonely stretch of highway at night, woods crowding the roadway, who sees a black shape moving just at the edge of her headlights? What of the teen hiking a trail in one of our forests that sees a flash of movement in the underbrush? What must they think?

For many city people, much of the wildlife they see is on the television, in a movie or perhaps in a city park. They often have a clear, unobstructed view or the filmmaker has made sure that the critter is centered in his footage. Nevertheless, it is not like that when you are in that creature's "house". Most times, you don't see the entire animal or you may see nothing more than a flash of gray fur as a coyote streaks away in the dense brush. That tall white being you see floating away from you in the distance isn't a white Sasquatch; it is the upright tail of a deer bounding away, maybe even an albino or piebald deer.

*Albino deer are about one per 30,000. Piebald deer may have large or small areas of white and are much more common yet still considered rare. Photograph; Sitka black-tailed deer (courtesy Brian & Aaron Bitz)*

I once took a break while hiking and sat down against a tree on the edge of a clearing. I had only been there a few minutes when I heard something walking behind me. It walked, then stopped, walked then stopped. I turned slowly around and there, not more than forty yards away was a nervous whitetail doe working her way past me just inside the brush line. I could see her as plain as day, prancing by with her tail up. Then she stopped, lowered her tail and I lost her. She simply melted away! I scanned the woods trying to figure out where she had gone but couldn't find her until she raised her tail again. She had never moved. By simply dropping her tail, she had blended so well with the background that I couldn't pick her out even though I was staring right at her. Had I been a neophyte without the patience to sit a while longer, would I have returned to the city with an extraordinary tale of the inter-dimensional deer that vanished before my eyes?

I don't know how many times I've had a deer sneak in and then stand, screened by brush, just staring at me. Some of these stand-offs have lasted for what seem hours but were probably just minutes. Unable to shoot for lack of positive identification of the target, afraid to move for fear of scaring it off, there's nothing to be done but wait. Finally, the deer wins and I move only to find that the black nose and white throat patch is nothing more than a bole on a birch tree. Of course, it has worked in reverse too. That gray upright sapling with the white bird flitting low in the branches is nothing to get excited about. So when I stand to stretch, imagine my surprise when the sapling turns out to be the deer's leg and the white bird was the deer twitching its ear?

We cannot always be sure that what we are looking at is what we are seeing. We are vision-oriented. We humans depend more on our sight than any of our other senses. Yet, our sight can let us down or rather, our mind does by misinterpreting what we see. If we go in the woods and expect to see the entire animal, we will miss the one that is screened by undergrowth. But it is there, our eyes see it, it's the mind that fouls up. We are not seeing what we expect to see; therefore, we see nothing at all, or worse, we see what isn't there. That eight-foot tall Bigfoot you saw staring menacingly at you before it turned and disappeared into another dimension, was actually a five foot black bear standing on its hind legs to sniff the air, unsure of what you are. The animal only seemed to disappear because it had dropped back to four legs and quietly snuck away.

I stood on a fencerow overlooking a cut cornfield one evening. It was almost too dark to shoot and I was getting ready to leave when from the woods behind me I heard a large flapping sound. I turned just in time to see the biggest bird of my life fly up into a tree. Was it a thunderbird? Some might have thought so. Of course, I knew there was only one of two things it might have been: a great horned owl carrying a mouse back to his roost to eat or a turkey getting ready for bed. I didn't have time to check it out as my partners were waiting for me at the truck. Since it was cold and I had the keys, I figured they were a priority. But what if I hadn't seen it? What if I had only heard it?

There is a quietness that descends on the woods at dusk, a transition period when the critters of the day punch out and the night shift starts. Sounds take on a clarity that wouldn't be noticed an hour earlier or an hour later. A mouse running through the leaf litter will make you think you're in Pamplona at the "Running of the Bulls". If it's cold enough, you can almost hear the sap freezing in the trees. Our sense of hearing is limited compared to other animals. To those city folks, such as me, who have been subjected to loud, intense noise for any length of time, it's even worse. In my case, too many years with headphones and Ted Nugent have left me with tinnitis (a ringing, buzzing or hissing of the ears that 50 million adults suffer from). Even though, I still depend on my ears when out hunting, yet cannot always be sure of exactly what it is I'm hearing, and more importantly, where the sound is coming from.

Once while on a deer stand at the base of a large oak tree overlooking flat land along the Sugar River I had crossed, a river that was actually more of a creek, and waiting for the late coming hunters to push the deer across the creek to me, I never expected to hear one approaching from behind. Sure enough, just after daybreak, I heard a solitary deer making its way to the creek somewhere behind me. It would take a few steps, pause, and then take a few more. It had the cautious quality of a buck. So I sat as still as the tree trunk I was nestled against, only allowing my eyes to scan as far to the sides as possible, my heart thumping in my chest like a drum solo. Suddenly, there it was! It was a big, fat fox squirrel out gathering breakfast.

I had misidentified the scurrying of the tree rat for the cautious footsteps of a deer. I've heard plenty of deer and plenty of squirrels. What of the individual who hasn't? Would he or she have heard a (*)shunka warak'in, stalking them? After all, surely a tiny squirrel couldn't possibly make that much noise, could it?

Recalling one cold Thanksgiving weekend night in the late 1990s, my uncle and I had just gotten to the truck after dark and were packing the rifles when we heard the most horrifying scream imaginable; shivers went up my back! It was close, it was loud and it was angry. At the time, I had never heard of Bigfoot vocalizations so that didn't cross my mind. My original thought was a cougar, although the authorities claim there is none in Michigan. Even now, years later, I've not positively identified this scream. Was it a Sasquatch, enraged that we were still hanging around in his 'living room'? Was it a misplaced cougar that came to Michigan for a visit? On the other hand, did I, as I now believe, simply have the rare pleasure of listening to the scream of the great horned owl?

How many people would have insisted they heard a Bigfoot screaming in rage? How many would have heard that squirrel and sworn that some large, unidentified creature had stalked them? What about the person who claims that something followed them through the woods, something they could never catch a glimpse of but could hear, stepping when they stepped, stopping when they stopped? Is it the Goatman, Mothman or perhaps the Jersey Devil? Surely, it must be something evil or of legend come to life. Maybe, just maybe it's nothing more than a whitetail deer following closely but cautiously behind you as you wander. I have had deer follow me out of the woods at night. They are really not very skittish and if they feel safe enough, would much rather know where you are than split for parts unknown. After all, you have invaded their turf and if you do not present an immediate danger, deer can be unbelievably nervy.

Our sense of smell is probably one of the worst in the animal kingdom. As a past smoker, mine is particularly bad, although I did find a squirrel I had just shot by smelling it. It had lived long enough to crawl under a deadfall of foliage. However, generally, any odors we detect must be powerful. Yet, while it may be the weakest of our senses, I've researched enough to know that odors can often elicit the strongest of memories. Odors such as freshly brewing coffee, frying bacon, our wife's perfume or the baby powder on the child we love are comforting while foul odors are something we avoid. We recoil when our nostrils are assaulted with the stench of a skunk, rotting flesh or ammonia and the smell of anything-burning causes an alarm reaction. A foul odor is bound to transform any encounter, especially one with an unidentified animal, into something ominous.

For a hunter, being able to correctly identify wildlife is crucial. You have to be able to properly identify the game you can legally take and guarantee it be done in a safe manner. If you're hunting in one of the western states,

(*Shunka warak'in, an unknown animal based on a mount and Indian legend that appears dog-like.)

can you tell the difference between a mule deer and a whitetail deer? Often, you not only have to identify the target species, but perhaps the sex of the animal as well. Can you differentiate between a cow and bull caribou? Both have antlers. The best way to accomplish this objective is to spend as much time in the woods as possible. Nothing replaces the experience of seeing live animals under natural conditions. Carrying good field guides can be a huge aid as well.

Next in importance is to spend time looking at pictures. The more pictures you can view, the better off you are. Try to find pictures taken from odd angles, or pictures of animals hidden by brush. Chances are, especially in eastern forests, you aren't going to see the entire animal. If you are going to target a specific area, look at not only the animals you will be hunting but also the ones you will not. It might prevent the accidental shooting of a protected animal. If you shoot an elk when deer are the legal game, it will not do you much good to claim you did not know elk also inhabited the area.

You might say, "But I'm hunting cryptids and there are no pictures." That is even more reason to become very familiar with the wildlife you may encounter in a given area. If there are black bears, where you're going to seek Sasquatch and you know this then know what black bears look like from various angles under different sighting conditions, thus properly identifying that tall dark shape as a bear, standing on its hind legs testing the winds scent instead of a mistaken anomalous Bigfoot-like creature.

The same can be said for sounds. Although this chapter is titled "The Silent Woods Around Us", the truth is the woods are anything but silent to those who listen. At times, they can be as noisy as any city environment. One of the problems I think some people have is that they are overwhelmed by just how noisy it can be. The sounds blend in together, running and mixing like paint until the sounds become nothing but, indiscriminate, meaningless white noise. But like the hum of city traffic signifying the vibrancy of the concrete jungle, think of it as the pulse of the wild. If you pick it apart, isolate the sounds, you hear a symphony of life. You need to listen, to take the pulse, for you'll hear far more than you'll see because there are tales to be told in that music and lessons to be learned. You hear those blue jays screaming in the distance? Over there, not more than a 150 yards off? They're screaming at something. It could be an owl they've discovered and decided to mob. So learn how species interact, blue jays aren't too fond of owls. Alternatively, could it be a Sasquatch making his way to that blueberry patch we passed a while ago. They do sound like they are coming this way, don't they? And just what is that gray squirrel barking at? What does he see? Something large just snapped a branch over there not far away. You can follow it with your ears my friend. It's coming this way.

You see how easy it is to build the vision. Hunt with your ears, as well as your sight. Listen to animal calls. Learn what animals might be found in the area you're searching. If you know you're going to be in an area that holds elk in early fall, that strange whistle with the grunts at the end will be recognizable as a rutting bull bugling his challenge to other bulls and not a Bigfoot screaming his rage at your intrusion.

Often, the animals you are going to see will be fleeing. Try as I might, there is no way I can get my 260 pounds through the woods as gracefully

144

and as quietly as even a bear who might weigh as much or twice what I weigh and the faster I move, the noisier I am. The trick of moving quietly is to move slowly. You should actually spend more time looking than moving. It isn't how much ground you cover that matters, it's how much ground you cover well. In fact, the best strategy is to find a likely spot and simply sit. Let the animals come to you. Place yourself in a good vantage point, a piece of high ground or along a well-used trail or creek crossing. If you must move, do so slowly. Take a few steps, stop and look around. I mean really look around. Pick that brush apart, branch-by-branch and leaf by leaf if you must. Do not expect to see the entire animal either. Look for movement. It may be simply a leaf twisting in the breeze, yet it could be a deer rotating its ear, or a squirrel flipping its tail or just maybe it might be that Ivory-billed woodpecker flitting from tree to tree.

If you're looking for cryptids, keep in mind that chances are, many of the rules that apply to hunting ordinary game animals will apply to cryptids as well. When you finally decide where you want to look, spend some time studying a topographic map. Most animals seek fringe cover, places where two or more different types of terrain or vegetation meet. Examples would be where swamp and high ground converge, second growth scrub butting up against old growth forest, a ridge running along a marsh. Variations in elevation are also edges. Sometimes the edges are well defined but other times, they may be more obscure. You will be able to find many of these spots simply by studying the map.

Make an educated guess as to what type of environment your cryptid quarry might prefer. It wouldprobably be a waste of time to search for a Thunderbird with a twenty-foot wingspan in a forest thick with undergrowth or an expanse of marshland with no trees to roost in. You would not search for Bigfoot in the Midwestern plains and you would not want to waste time looking for a giant amphibian miles from any water source. Or would you?

Don't make the mistake of thinking that you need to hit only the heavy cover to find your elusive quarry. Sure, it may be bedded down in the thickest cover within a given area, but chances are that when it moves, it will take the path of least resistance. Will a Bigfoot push its way through the tightest tangle it can find when it can move through an area using established trails? What would you do? Exactly right. Bigfoot will take the easy way, as most animals will because for them energy is not found as easy as a trip to the corner market.

As you're looking, make sure you're seeing. Many people look at the trees and never beyond or through. It's a little more difficult when the trees and shrubs are leafed but you can get some great practice, believe it or not in the winter, and of all places, on the road. As you drive by a woodlot in your car practice looking through the trees not at them. See how far into the woods you can actually see. As a truck driver, I do this daily. It helps me learn to look not at the tree trunks but between them, around them and past them. Being in motion you'll notice the perspective of the ground change as you drive by, making it easier than if you were stationary. However, the principle is the same. The old saying about not seeing the forest for the trees is all too true. So what should we be looking for? Look for horizontal lines. Woods are vertically oriented. Trees grow upright. A horizontal line will more times than not, simply be a fallen tree. Nevertheless, it might be the back of a deer, or coyote or maybe even that shunka warak'in you are searching for and hope to find. This might not help much with Bigfoot, a vertically oriented biped, but it is still a good method for spotting and orienting yourself to the scenery. Bigfoot supposedly bends, twists and breaks branches and even small trees so this technique can help in identifying such anomalies.

Check out anything that seems out of place or a little odd, such as a blotch of color that seems wrong or a strange shape. Ask yourself if that bulge in the tree is an old nest or is it a perching bird? Look for contrasts. If you're searching a stand of aspens or birch, a light colored environment, look closely at dark spots. The converse is true if searching darker areas. Most times it will turn out to be nothing more than a stump, a bole on a tree, maybe a little cluster of reddish maple leaves that somehow hung on through the winter but study and understand what it is you're seeing.

Movement of any kind should always be investigated. It may be nothing more than a leaf blowing in the breeze, a squirrel flicking its tail in that nervous way they do or a bird flitting among the branches. Anytime I see movement I cannot immediately identify, I freeze (become a tree as the Indian's say) and concentrate on it. Sometimes it helps to look just a little to the side of whatever it is you're trying to identify and use your peripheral vision. If you still cannot identify it, *slowly* change your position to gain a slightly different perspective. It may make all the difference.

While our sense of smell may not be much to brag about, a few days in the wilds should improve it somewhat. No, we will never be able to match our wild friends, but you would be surprised what you can sniff out if you pay attention. I have smelled swamp water before I came close to getting my feet wet and sniffed out berry patches. I have heard of hunters who can smell a herd of elk from a far distance or picked up a fresh scent of a fern hollow two klicks ahead. What you might smell depends on how well your nose is and how well you learn to pay attention to it's messages.

Perhaps a more important consideration when it comes to smell is to remember that almost invariably your quarry, if you are not careful is going to smell you first. Walk into the wind whenever possible. Remember that as air warms, it rises. If you are working your way up a ridge in the morning, your odor is going to drift up alerting anything there. The opposite is true in the evening, as the air cools it floats downward.

If you're going to hunt cryptids, bring them back alive or captured on film. If you must go armed, either to collect a specimen or simply for protection, be well acquainted with the game laws of the state or province and area. The laws can vary greatly, not only from state to state and province to province but from area to area within a given state or province. These laws can sometimes be complex and if you have any questions, contact the game department of the area you expect to explore.

Every year hundreds of people die outdoors needlessly, usually from exposure or accident but most of this can be avoided with a little planning, precaution and common sense. There are many sources of information on what should and should not be done when trekking through wilderness areas. If it is all new to you, start out small, with a few day hikes into a state park and never alone. I would not advise a neophyte to take a week or month long backpacking trip into the interior of Alaska if he or she has not spent a single night in a tent. I've hunted since I was a youngster in Michigan, done woods traipsing in Tennessee and hiked in Ontario and with that under my belt I wouldn't think of setting off on a solo backpacking trip in Alaska or one of the truly wilderness areas of our great western states myself. Be aware of your limitations, respect nature for she can be unforgiving. If you set reasonable, educated boundaries there is no reason to not step back to that time when we were all a little closer to nature.

Who knows? Some night you might be sitting around that campfire, staring into the flames in that magic, hypnotic trance of the campfire, as you listen to the crackle and watch the popping of the flames, soon feeling that energy drain from a days hike, thinking in that dream-like state that precedes sleep of the twisted sapling you found that morning. Recalling that strange hair wedged in the bark of that old cedar tree on the edge of that gloomy swamp you poked around during the afternoon. Wondering if something other than raccoons might finally feed on those apples you left on that stump on the other side of the clearing. Then, just as the flames give way to glowing coals and the thoughts of your sleeping bag really begin to take hold in your mind, you notice the crickets fall silent, the snap of a large branch echoes against the tent, over there, just inside the tree line is a hint of rotting flesh and wet dog smell that tickles your nostrils. You reach for another dried branch to throw on the fire wishing you hadn't left your flashlight in the tent as your eyes pierce the darkness, following the shadow moving among shadows........

Remember, the journey is the destination, immerse yourself in the total experience.

Gerry Bacon's common sense observations of his experiences, which encompass the need to utilize every aspect of one's senses and requires first and foremost a logical reasoning of events, are without a doubt Cryptozoology and the paranormal's best friends. To scientifically evaluate the events around you, thus removing all assumptions and maintaining a high level of awareness, will only enhance the true "unknown" stories yet to be told.

Many adventures await the daring and many unknown encounters are revealed to those who demand an answer. Seeking and investigating a legitimat,e undiscovered animal or ghostly entity is a rarity, not to be found in every shadow or whistling wind. This interest in the strange is a unique one --- made even more so by the fact that sometimes when answers are found, they are not always understood.

# ADDENDUM: CRYPTO-CELEBRATION
## A Culinary Delight by Robert Coppen

**T**he following tongue-in-cheek piece by novelist Robert Coppen expresses his own crypto-twist with his own taste- tested terrific recipes. Enjoy!

So, you want to go on an expedition to find a cryptid? Have the urge to wander around in the woods, looking for Bigfoot? Want to head out into the cypress swamps, in search of the elusive ivory-billed woodpecker? Feel like sitting on the shores of Loch Ness with your spotting scope in hand, scanning the loch for the fabulous Nessie? Good for you! After all, what better way is there to spend your vacation than looking for unknown animals? Personally, I can't think of any. I'd much rather be standing knee-deep in a mosquito-infested swamp, looking for Mokele-Mbembe, than lazing on the beach at the Riviera, any day.

But, no matter what cryptid you're looking for, you're going to have to fuel the engine in the process. The engine of your body, that is. And your body's engine requires food and drink, doesn't it? But what kind of food and drink? Ordinary food and drink? I think not. After all, looking for a cryptid is far from an ordinary endeavor. And just as we often pair a good meal with a fine wine when dining out in a fancy restaurant, so should we do the same when searching for cryptids. Just imagine what a letdown it would be to have finally gotten that oh-so-elusive proof of that oh-so-elusive Bigfoot, only to have nothing with you to celebrate the occasion other than a box of Minute Rice and a can of Schlitz! The mind boggles! The sensibilities reel! Isn't it much better to be prepared for such an eventuality with a nice T-bone steak and a bottle of Sierra Nevada's Bigfoot Barley Wine Ale? Now, that's a celebratory meal! And what about Nessie, should you finally obtain proof of her existence? A packet of Ramen Pride noodles and a pint of Mr. Boston vodka? Heck no! If you find Nessie, you'll be in Scotland, won't you? So how about a heaping serving of that traditional Scottish dish, Haggis, washed down with the whisky of whiskies, the one-and-only, smoky and peaty Glenlivet? Doesn't that sound much more interesting? And surely Nessie deserves the best you can give her, doesn't she? I think so. I know so.

So, with the above in mind, just how do you go about doing this? First, your cryptid hunting expedition is preferably going to be one that has a base camp, one with a refrigerator, or at least an ice box. You can't take steak with you on a backpacking trip, any more than you can keep your beer cold while doing the same. So, you need a cabin or a rental cottage, or something along those lines. A log cabin is usually the best option for most cryptids, seeing as how there's just something about a log cabin that fits in so well with any type of wilderness endeavor. Then you can go out during the day, wandering around in the woods and swamps or scanning large bodies of water, feeling secure that, if you do find a cryptid critter, you will have the proper food and drink back at your base camp to celebrate the momentous occasion with. And you should learn how to barbecue, since looking for cryptids is most definitely a barbecuing endeavor, and not a souffle and quiche-making one. And you should learn how to barbecue with wood, or perhaps charcoal briquets, instead of just using a gas grill, because the flavor of your food will be so much better. Actual wood coals are the best. Trust me on this.

So, how to barbecue? It's not all that difficult, really. Basically, you start your fire with your wood and let it burn down to a nice even bed of coals. Then you put your food on top of a grill over the coals and cook it. What could be simpler? Of course it's not quite that simple, but you get the basic idea. But there's a few things to keep in mind, especially safety precautions:

1) Don't burn down the woods. This means to make certain that, if you build an actual fire, as opposed to using a grill, you should always use a fire pit, whether you build it yourself or use a prepared fire ring. Make sure you remove all leaves and other debris from the area of the pit and line it with rocks. Put the fire out thoroughly when you're finished. Use plenty of water. Don't be careless. Follow the rules of the area you're in and make sure you have the proper permits, if they're needed (and they usually are).

2) Never take wood from standing trees. Use dead ones that have fallen to the ground, instead. But don't use dead wood that's laying directly on the ground, as it will invariably be too damp to burn well.

3) Be careful with your charcoal lighter fluid. Don't pour it directly on the fire once it's started: the fire can run up the stream of fluid and burn you or maybe even cause the can of fluid to explode in your hand.

4) If you don't have a cabin and are backpacking, put your food in a duffel bag and tie it up in a tree, out of the reach of bears, unless of course you're not in bear country. Change the clothes you cooked in and put them up in the tree, too. Make sure the tree is a good distance away from your camping spot. Of course, having a cabin will make this unnecessary. And a cabin is a good place to keep a refrigerator, well supplied with beer.

5) Be polite. You bring it in with you, take it out with you. Don't litter. Respect others.

But, you say, I can't afford to rent a cabin. Does this mean I'm destined to be eating backpacking food only, like dried soup and stuff like that? Heck no! You just have to learn the area you're going cryptid hunting in. I, personally, have been hunting for cryptids for years, with the cryptids I'm hunting for being those mysterious black panthers that have been reported all over the US, Britain and Australia. And I can't afford to rent a cabin, either. My area is upstate NY and I concentrate on two different places: the Moose River Plains in the Adirondack Mountains, and the Charles T. Baker State Forest in Brookfield, NY. Both areas have miles and miles of dirt roads running through them, with camping areas complete with fire rings that are accessible by car. And both are very wild areas, with reports of black panthers and/or eastern cougars coming from them. Have I ever seen one? Nope, but I have had a lot of fun looking for the critters, and have seen a lot of other types of interesting wildlife in the process. And you can do the same. It just takes a little research. You too can hunt for cryptids in your own backyard, and enjoy some fine outdoor meals while you're doing so. And what could be better than that? And now, on to the recipes and the beer....

## Cryptid Beverages & Some Foods to Pair with Them

Please don't expect this part to read like a cookbook. If you do, you'll be disappointed, and who wants that? After all, and to be honest, I'm not a cook and hardly know what I'm doing in the kitchen. Not my area. So if I can do it, so can you. Oh, and don't expect there to be any measuring going on, either. None of that "Use 1.375 teaspoons" stuff, for me. I don't even own a measuring cup, actually.

Now, on to the first cryptid beverage (and the food that goes with it):

### Bigfoot Barley Wine Ale and Steak

So, you've been traipsing around in the forests of the Pacific Northwest, on the hunt for Patti. And you've managed to take some photographs. And there was film in the camera and you took the lens cap off and everything. And you're hungry and thirsty and want something good to celebrate the momentous occasion with. Try this:

Build your fire (or light your charcoal briquets). After it's burned down to a nice hot bed of coals, oil the grill with a little olive oil (or the vegetable oil of your choice), grab a bottle of Bigfoot and pour it into a beer glass; if you drink it out of the bottle, you'll lose the aroma. Smell it. Sip it. Savor it. Now wasn't that good? You bet it was! A nice big, malty, hoppy, high abv (alcohol by volume) brew with tons of flavor and pizazz. This is what you want to help you celebrate your obtaining proof of bigfoot's existence! Not that insipid, boring, fizzy yellow stuff that's mass-produced to appeal to the non-cryptid enthusiasts of the world and is loaded with chemicals and adjuncts, as well as being totally unloaded with flavor. Never! And what kind of food goes well with Bigfoot? Steak, is what. Nothing better, in my opinion. And a simple steak is best, too. And simple is good, out in the woods.

Now that you're warmed up and ready for the grilling, grab your steak. You can use any kind of steak you want: Sirloin, Porterhouse, T-bone, Rib-eye, Filet Mignon, London broil * it doesn't matter (but Rib-eye is the tenderest): everything tastes good on a camping trip. Especially when it's washed down with an ale like Bigfoot. Just try to keep your steaks in the area of 1 to 1.5 inches thick. Much thinner and they'll burn too easy, much thicker and it'll take too long to cook 'em.

Okay, now here's the hard part: toss the steak on the grill.

Scary, wasn't it? Okay, now you just sit and wait, sippin' on your Bigfoot and reveling in your cryptid-catching triumph for a while. How long should you wait, you ask? About five minutes, I answer, and then you flip the steak over. Wait another five minutes or so, and you're done. Except for the salt and pepper, and the knife and fork. And another glass of Bigfoot Barley Wine Ale. Cheers!

*Note: Be careful not to overcook the steak. There's nothing worse than a burnt-to-a-crisp, dry-as-a-bone steak. It doesn't go well with any kind of beer or cryptid. And that's the truth.*

### All-Purpose Cryptid Veggies

You really don't want your ale and steak to get lonely, do you? Of course not! They should have company, and you should eat your veggies, too (do I sound like your mother?). And besides, this is easy:

Rip off a piece of tinfoil about two feet long and lay it down on a flat surface. Rip off another one the same size and lay it down perpendicular to the other so the two of them make a heavy "cross" of sorts. Wash (or rinse off or whatever) a couple of big potatoes and chop'em up and dump'em in the middle of the "cross." Do the same with a bell pepper or two (get rid of the seeds). Add one small hot pepper* (really get rid of the seeds). Avoid habaneros unless you really like heat. Cut up an ear of corn into two or three-inch pieces and toss the pieces on top of the taters and peppers. Dump some olive oil on top of the whole thing. Add some Adobo (spice mix made by Goya: salt, pepper, turmeric, garlic and oregano). Fold up two ends of the "cross" so you've got a bag of veggies, open at two ends. Fold up a third end so you've got a bag of veggies, open at one end. Pour about a third of an average size bottle of beer into the bag. Bigfoot Barley Wine Ale works just fine. Drink the rest of the beer. Fold up the last side of the bag of veggies so there aren't any open ends and toss the bag on the grill. Start this before you start your steak (or whatever) because it takes about 45 minutes to cook. Steaming the veggies, is what your doing, and not grilling'em. You can check'em every once in a while, if you want, simply by peeling back a little of the tin foil and stabbing'em with a fork. The potatoes take the longest, so when your fork goes into a potato easily (*) you're done. Or you can just sit and wait and drink beer. This is what I usually do, personally. And it's worth the wait, because these are good. Go well with almost any beer and almost any food. Just don't forget to pour some beer into the bag of veggies or you'll burn'em, and they're not much good then.

(*) Note: If you don't really want to bother with genuine hot peppers you can just use some Tabasco (or the hot sauce of your choice). It's up to you.

Also, when handling real hot peppers you should make sure you wash your hands thoroughly afterwards, and don't rub your eyes before you do. Or take a leak. I'm not kidding here.

### *Dixie Blackened Voodoo Lager & Barbecued Ribs*

The southern U.S. is a hotspot for those mysterious "black panther" sightings that fascinate us all so much. I have no idea why there seems to be so many more of the critters down south, as opposed to up north, but there you go: big black kitty cats with glowing red eyes are sighted practically every weekend, away down south in Dixie. And nothing says "Deep South" better than barbecue, especially a rack of barbecued ribs. And a bottle of Blackened Voodoo Lager to wash it down with.

So, after you've spent the day interviewing any and all locals who've spotted the beasties and have been escorted by them to the various places where they saw the critters and have walked around in the woods all on your lonesome, looking for tracks, and maybe actually saw and photographed one and have returned to your camp and finished writing it all down in your journal in one huge run-on sentence, build a fire or light your charcoal briquets.

And make sure the coals are hot. Sure, smoked and slow-cooked ribs are good, but wood coals or charcoal briquets might not stay lit long enough to cook ribs that way. Make the coals glow hot and red, just like the eyes of the "black panthers" do. And keep the grill close to the coals, too. But before you even get started, you should have had your ribs marinating overnight in some soppin' sauce in anticipation of your success. There are all sorts of good marinades out there, or you can make your own. Heres one simple recipe:

Dump some ketchup in a saucepan, maybe three cups or so. Throw in some Worcestershire, maybe half a coffee cup full. Add about the same amount of cider vinegar (or very dry hard cider). Salt and tabasco and cayenne to taste. A couple of minced garlic cloves. A little bit of very strong coffee. And finally, a little olive oil. Stir the whole mess up and bring to a boil on the stove. Then simmer for 20 minutes or so. You will probably get about four cups out of this, which you can refrigerate for a few weeks.

Okay, now that your fire has burned down to some very hot coals, you can get to work. First thing you do is grab a bottle of Dixie Blackened Voodoo Lager and open it. Pour it into a glass. Note the dark brown body of the beer, lit up with ruby highlights. Admire the brownish head and the malty aroma. Drink it. Smooth and creamy, isn't it? And tasty, with nuances of bread and sweet malts, mixed in with just enough hops to balance. Ahhh!

Now you get out your rack of ribs, which you split into two halves and put in the marinade the night before. Toss each half-rack onto the grill and lean back, sipping on your beer and reveling in your crypto-hunting success. Get up every once in a while to brush some more sauce on the ribs and to flip'em over. Cooking time is going to vary here, since you're using a wood fire (or charcoal briquets). You want them to be tender and cooked all the way through, and the only way to really tell is to check them with a knife or fork every once in a while. Expect the cooking time to be somewhere around half-an-hour, though, or maybe even a bit less (or more), depending on how hot your coals are. If you're using a grill with a lid, close the lid when you're not checking the ribs to speed up the cooking time. And expect to go through maybe two or three beers while you're waiting for the ribs to cook. Or more, even.

When the ribs are done, dig in, keeping them company with another bottle of Dixie Blackened Voodoo Ale and some grilled corn on the cob.

### Cryptid Grilled Corn on the Cob

Easy one, this is. Take the husks and silk off as many ears of sweet corn as you want to eat. Melt some butter in a saucepan over your hot coals. Dump into the melted butter some mixed Italian seasoning: oregano, basil, etc. Brush the melted butter and seasoning over your ears of corn and put'em on the grill. Turn'em every once in while with tongs. In 10 minutes or so they will be done, and nicely browned. Season with salt and pepper to taste and enjoy with your barbecued ribs and another Dixie Blackened Voodoo Lager. Yum!

### Worm-in-the-Bottle Tequila and Hot n' Spicy Grilled Tortillas

After months of research, you've decided to bite the big one and go after the most controversial cryptid of all: the famous and infamous Chupacabra, the old Latin American goatsucker. You've decided where to go (someplace in Mexico, or perhaps Puerto Rico) and have contacted a goat rancher, who has agreed, for a few pesos and the promise that you won't burn down the chaparral (or cactus, or jungle, or grass, or whatever) that covers his land, to let you camp on his property and keep an eye on his goats and to shoot any chupas that might attack them. Your camp is set up (in this case a tent) and you've got your rifle and your camera and your night vision goggles and your scope. It's a clear night. The stars are out and the owls are hooting and the goats are grazing and the chupacabras are out there: you know they are. And you're ready to rock-n-roll.

So, just in case you do manage to bag one of the bloodsuckers, what should your food and drink be to celebrate the occasion? Burgers and beer? Of course not! Mexico isn't known for good beer, Corona fans to the contrary, and a burger is a bit too plebeian to celebrate the killing or capture (or photographing) of such a famous and extraordinary cryptid as El Chupa. Forget about the hot dogs, as well, since there are many people who think that Chupacabras are nothing more than feral dogs roaming the Latin American countryside, killing goats and sheep and chickens willy-nilly. Cook up some dogs and all you might see are dogs: hunting magic, just like the cave paintings at Lascaux. And you, of course, know perfectly well that Chupacabras are not feral dogs. After all, dogs don't suck all the blood out of their victims through two puncture wounds, as chupas are wont to do. So, and anyway, if it's not going to be burgers or dogs and beer, what is it going to be? Try this:

After you've spent a good amount of time admiring your strange catch

--- staring in fascination at its wings and kangaroo-ish legs and bulging reptilian eyes and humanoid arms, or whatever in the heck features it actually has (descriptions vary) * build yourself a fire, or light the charcoal briquets in your hibachi, the most portable of all the barbecue grills, and let the flames die down to hot coals. While you're waiting, open up a bottle of tequila and slice up a lime, making certain you have a salt shaker handy. Be sure to use the real deal tequila, the stuff that actually has a worm in the bottle, because it'll add to the ambience. Shake a little salt on one of your hands, have yourself a shot of the tequila, bite on a lime slice and lick the salt off your hand. Repeat. Simple and good and oh so appropriate to your surroundings. And, who knows, it might help your night vision, thereby increasing your chances of spotting another one of those elusive chupas. After all, the vast majority of Chupacabra sightings come from places where tequila is the adult beverage of choice. Is this a coincidence? I think not.

Anyway, when the wood or charcoal has turned to glowing coals, brush a little olive oil on your grill and put it over the fire. Throw some meat on the grill, perhaps some goat meat or mutton, provided by the rancher on whose land you're camping. Take some flour tortillas (which you've cadged off the wife of the same rancher who provided you with the meat) and brush some olive oil on'em. Chop up an onion and a few hot peppers, making sure to remove any seeds from the hot peppers. Put the onions and peppers on a perforated grill pan and slather 'em with a little olive oil. Put the onion-and-pepper laden grill pan on the grill. Turn the veggies every once in a while with a wooden spoon or a spatula. When the goat meat is almost finished, put the oiled tortillas on the grill. Remove the tortillas from the grill as soon as they start to puff up a bit. Chop up the goat meat and dump it on the tortillas. You'll need a work surface for this, like a big flat rock or something. Dump the cooked onions and the hot peppers on top of the meat. Dump some feta cheese on top of the veggies (I know, feta cheese is a Greek thing, and not a Latin American thing, but who wants to be a fanatic?). Fold the tortillas over and toss 'em back on the grill until the cheese melts. Remove the folded-over tortillas and cut into wedges like pizza slices. Sit back and relax and enjoy your meal. If you can stand the heat of the peppers, punctuate with an occasional tequila-lime-salt interlude. Trust me, this is a meal you'll never forget; much more memorable than anything any of those poor deluded souls who are not interested in cryptids can ever hope to enjoy in even the most expensive of restaurants. Cheers!

### Davidson Brothers IPA and Lake "Champ"-plain Brook Trout

Okay, so now you've rented a cabin on the shore of Lake Champlain and have just spent the day searching for "Champ," America's version of "Nessie," the famous Loch Ness monster. You've got yourself a boat and a camera with a telephoto lens and have been out all day, looking for the beastie. And you've taken some photographs, photographs which you are pretty darned sure are not of an otter, or a wave, or a loon, or of anything other than Champ herself. So, since Champ is a water beastie, maybe you should celebrate by cooking up a water beastie. In this case, a brook trout, which you just might be able to catch yourself, pulling it out of the waters of the lake (assuming it's fishing season and you have a fishing license). And no fish is more representative of the Northeast than the brook trout. Or tastier.

This is a frying pan job, and not really a grill job, but it's probably the best way to cook trout (truit en bleu not excepted). And it's easy. And it pairs well with Davidson Brother's IPA, which is a somewhat unusual India Pale Ale, made with Ringwood yeast, a yeast which imparts distinctive "butterscotch" notes to any beer made with it. Most IPA's would overpower trout with a plethora of hops, but this one is subtle and balanced enough to work with trout quite well. And Davidson Brothers is an upstate New York microbrewery and Champ is an upstate New York (and Vermont) cryptid.

Anyway, put a big frying pan over your very hot coals (or even flames) and fry up some bacon to whatever degree of crispness you want. Remove the bacon and put aside on a paper towel to drain. Add enough vegetable oil to the bacon grease still in the pan until the level of oil in the pan is approximately half-an-inch deep. Take your brook trout, which you've either caught and cleaned yourself or purchased in a fish market and kept on ice in the fridge, and dredge it in some yellow corn meal until a dusting of corn meal covers the trout. Open the trout up and place it in the hot and bubbling oil. Leave it for about four minutes and then flip over. After another four minutes or so it should be done. This is for a nine-inch trout, sans head and tail. The bigger and thicker the trout the longer it will take per side to cook. Up to six minutes per side for an 11-incher. Just check it once in a while, since the best way to ruin fish is to overcook it.

Put the trout on a plate, add a little salt and pepper if you want, cover it with the bacon strips, and eat it along with some cryptid all-purpose veggies, all washed down with a glass of the Davidson Brothers IPA. Or maybe two glasses. Or three. And lean back and relax, and look out over Lake Champlain marveling at how lucky you are to have the chance to be near such an amazing and elusive creature as the Lake Champlain monster. A toast to Champ! And to many more cryptid-hunting expeditions. Cheers!

### Thunderbird Drunken Chicken and Storm King Imperial Stout

This one's a little different from the rest, since you'll probably need a gas grill for it, which means you'll need a rental cabin (or one you own, yourself). Actually, you can use a wood fire or a charcoal grill, but a gas grill is much easier. Either way, it'll be worth it. I promise. And so will the cryptid it goes with: the incredible Thunderbird, the flashing-eyed, monstrous-winged bird of Native American legend and lore.

And where do you go to look for the Thunderbird? Why, in the Thunderbird Mecca, of course --- Pennsylvania's Black Forest region. Where else? For decades people have been reporting huge raptors with 20-foot wingspans from that area. Some have even seen the creatures fly off with adult white-tailed deer! Pretty scary, isn't it? Fascinating, too. And there's simply no reason why you, too, can't get a glimpse of these incredible birds. Perhaps you'll even manage to get a good photo or find a feather or maybe even, gasp! A carcass!

So you've spent the entire day on top of a fire tower in one of the state forests that are scattered throughout this area of northern Pennsylvania, scanning the skies with your binoculars for one of the beasties. And you've even seen one, with its immense black wings spanning the skies and its monstrously beaked head scanning the forests for prey. And you're hoping you're not the prey. And it's the most amazing thing you've ever seen. And you even managed to take a photo. And you're suddenly very hungry and thirsty. And .... on to the recipe:

Fire up your gas grill. Set it to medium-high. Take a whole chicken and spice up its innards any way you like. I use Adobo and Caribbean Jerk Seasoning (cayenne, sugar, allspice, thyme, onion and salt), but you can use whatever in the heck you want. Open a can of beer, any beer, and drink a third of it. Stuff the can of beer, containing the remaining two-thirds of the beer, in the chicken --- ouch! --- and stand the chicken up on the grill, using its legs to make a tripod so it'll stay standing up. Close the lid on the grill. Wait two hours or so. Voila! The beer will evaporate and soak into the chicken, makin' it the moistest, tenderest bird you ever sunk your teeth into!

Now, to drink with this concoction, just any beer will most certainly not do. My suggestion is Storm King Imperial Stout, a monstrously good beer made in Pennsylvania by Victory, a highly regarded microbrewery. A giant beer (9% abv.) to accompany a whole beer-soaked chicken to commemorate the sighting of a giant bird. What could be more appropriate? Even the beer bottle's label is symbolic of the event, with it's flashing-eyed black raptor staring you in the face. And the flavor? Yowzah! Practically legendary, just like its namesake's existence. So cut yourself a slice of Drunken Chicken and pour yourself a glass of black-as-night Storm King, and toast your sighting of the most magnificent bird not known to science: the fabulous Thunderbird.

Remember, if you use a wood fire or a charcoal grill, keep in mind that you'll still need to cover the bird while it's cooking and that you'll have to add more wood or charcoal after an hour or so of cooking time. And be careful not to spill hot beer on yourself when removing the chicken from the grill, regardless of which type of grill you use. And, regardless of which cryptid you're hunting for, have fun! Cheers!

# ACKNOWLEDGMENTS

I hardly know where to begin in thanking the many people and organizations for their assistance, contributions, inspiration and even, at times, for their patience. I do hope that no one has been overlooked at this writing but if by chance I do, be sure you are no less appreciated.

First a special heartfelt thank you to Jennifer Lynne, Jessica, Jamie, Hayden and Ben. Also as equal, a special loving thank you to Tammy, Nick and Tara Coleman.

I'd like to take this opportunity to publicly tip my hat (again) to the contributions to this book of Cathy Clark of California, Gerry Bacon of Michigan, Robert Coppen author of "The Diary of Justin Hunter" (www.riverdream.com) of New York, Paul Schuman of Virginia and the devoted research, investigations and insight of Deborah Kaye Shira of North Carolina.

Again, thanks to the assistance received from universities, Tennessee agencies, newspaper publications, The Rogersville Veterinary Clinic, Rogersville, TN, the Church Hill police department, Church Hill, TN and the New Orleans police department, LA. I also owe a special research thanks to Cisco Serret, Will Duncan, the late Mark Chorvinsky, Bill Scott, Troy Taylor and Mike Nimmons. Additionally my sincere gratitude is extended to the numerous witnesses and scores of landowners for their contributions and cooperation.

I wish to acknowledge and thank these group members which are too numerous to name as individual's for their inspiration and continued support ; Cryptozoology.com, Cryptozoology USA, Cryptids Unlimited, The Crypto-Network and The East Tennessee Paranormal Society.

My first book "Strange Highways" brought about unique, rewarding and fantastic personal experiences. I would like to thank all of the people who took their time to come to the book signings, university sponsored events, e-mailed comments and further encouraged the writing of this book you now hold.

Sincerely,
Jerry D. Coleman

# ABOUT THE AUTHOR
## By Tammy Sheree Christian

Jerry D. Coleman was born October 3, 1951 in Decatur, Illinois. He is the third son of four children born to father firefighter Loren Coleman Sr. (1921-1985) and Chickamauga Cherokee mother, Anna McClain (1927- ). A childhood of self-preservation brought about the necessity to escape and survive through explorations into the dark of night and thick of forests. His early encounters of a possible UFO observed in 1961 and the 1962 discovery of a believed ape track put Coleman on a path to the unknown. It was in these early years of family turmoil that Jerry's interest turned to Cryptozoology and the paranormal, oddly seeking normality in the unknown from a known reality of abnormality.

Coleman now a father of four makes his home in east Tennessee's scenic Goshen Valley. An extremely rural location he has chosen to actively pursue his Cryptozoological and paranormal interests. A place teeming within a stones throw of Skunk Ape reports, Phantom Panther encounters, Ivory-billed woodpecker territory, Civil War battlefield ghosts, slave spirit history, phantom light phenomena and isolated, rarely trekked upon Appalachian Mountain wilderness. It is a location he chose with the sole purpose to actively pursue his field research.

The devotion to his research far surpasses his pulling up stakes and relocating. I have watched him spend hours on end and days turning into years as he researched and developed the investigation of his latest project, whether that project was a fleeting unusual sighting or a claimed cryptid report. His investigations entails months chasing down witnesses, scouring the backwoods and going door to door or forest to forest in search of further evidence or added testimony. Coleman leaves no stone unturned, every neighborhood, police station, newsroom and expert relevant to the encounters are tapped for information. The findings of his latest investigations are then communicated to trusted associates for their insight and often times jointly investigated. Coleman's quest for answers is unstoppable, never does he merely check out an encounter then shelf it. He devotes serious, repeated, in depth passion to it, yet at the same time, refuses to "bark up" an exhausted tree where only controversy or dead ends remain. Forever persistent as an investigator, Jerry Coleman publicly presents evidence in an open, honest and thorough manner to be judged, scrutinized and placed on the table for you to deliberate and evaluate on your individual plateau. These qualities of a comprehensive investigation bring his  expertise to an admired level in his field. So if you demand the truth, long for logic and expect an unbiased report, Coleman supplies it.

Jerry also wrote the popular 2003 Whitechapel release, "Strange Highways". His book, radio appearances and article contributions have been widely acclaimed as, "The standard for research in the unexplained!"

Tammy Sheree Christian

# ABOUT WHITECHAPEL PRODUCTIONS PRESS

Whitechapel Productions Press is a small publisher, specializing in books about ghosts and hauntings. Since 1993, the company has been one of America's leading publishers of supernatural books and has produced such best-seeling titles as "Haunted Illinois", "The Ghost Hunter's Guidebook" and many others. With nearly a dozen different authors producing high quality books on all aspects of ghosts, hauntings and the paranormal, Whitechapel Press has made its mark with America's ghost enthusiasts.

You can visit Whitechapel Productions Press online and browse through our selection of ghostly titles, plus get information on ghosts and hauntings, haunted history, spirit photographs, information on ghost hunting and much more. by visiting the internet website at:

## www.historyandhauntings.com

Whitechapel Press is the main company for some of the most acclaimed ghost tours in the country. We are the hosts for the following:

### History & Hauntings Ghost Tours of Alton, Illinois
Created by Troy Taylor, there tours are an interactive experience that allow readers to visit the historically haunted locations of the city and can be booked every year from April through October.

### Bump in the Night Ghost Tours
Created by authors Troy Taylor & Ursula Bielski, these tours offer Haunted Overnight Excursions to ghostly places around the Midwest and throughout the country. Available all year round!

### Chicago Hauntings Ghost Tours
Created by Ursula Bielski, these are the most authentic ghost tours in the Windy City and take readers to Chicago's most haunted sites. Available all year round!

Information on our books and tours are available on the website.

Printed in the United States
89809LV00001B/71/A

9 781892 523426